"If only a fraction of what is already known about the effects of sugar were to be revealed in relation to any other material used as a food additive, that material would promptly be banned . . ."

These are the words of Dr. John Yudkin, M.D., Ph.D., Professor of Physiology at Queen Elizabeth College of London University from 1945 to 1954 and Professor of Nutrition and Dietetics from 1954 to 1971. Now, Dr. Yudkin reveals the results of his own extensive research into the effects of ordinary table sugar on animals and human beings and explains why the sugar you eat—an astounding average of two pounds per person, per week —is not only entirely unnecessary physiologically, but deadly dangerous as well.

SWEET AND DANGEROUS

SWEET AND DANGEROUS

"Important . . . a significant contribution to popular thinking on nutrition."

"Professor Yudkin is well recognized as a distinguished authority on diet and nutrition . . . His approach is original and he writes with simplicity and conciseness."

Sweet and Dangerous

The new facts about the sugar you eat as a cause
of heart disease, diabetes, and other killers

John Yudkin, M.D.

BANTAM BOOKS
TORONTO · LONDON
NEW YORK

SWEET AND DANGEROUS

*A Bantam Book / published by arrangement with
Peter H. Wyden, Inc.*

PRINTING HISTORY

*Wyden edition published April 1972
2nd printing .... July 1972
Rodale Press Book Club edition published 1972
Bantam edition published May 1973
2nd printing*

*Bantam Books are published by Bantam Books, Inc., a National
General company. Its trade-mark, consisting of the words "Bantam
Books" and the portrayal of a bantam, is registered in the United
States Patent Office and in other countries. Marca Registrada.
Bantam Books, Inc., 666 Fifth Avenue, New York, N.Y. 10019.*

PRINTED IN THE UNITED STATES OF AMERICA

To
BENJAMIN
and
RUTH

Contents

Sweet and Dangerous

Why This Book
Is Necessary for
Your Health

There are several reasons why this was an opportune time for me to have written this book. First, my research on coronary disease has convinced me beyond doubt that sugar plays a considerable part in this terrifying modern epidemic. Secondly, many people have begun to question the highly publicized view that the principal culprit in this disease is the fat in our diet. Thirdly, a scientific symposium on the properties of sugar organized two years ago by myself as nutritionist, together with the professor of botany and the professor of chemistry at Queen Elizabeth College of London University, brought home to the three of us the enormous versatility and unique properties of the substance that is such a commonplace in all our lives.

These properties tie in all too neatly with the increasing evidence pointing to the involvement of sugar in many diseases, not just the coronary epidemic.

Much of the experimental work that I shall cite here was carried out in the department of nutrition at Queen Elizabeth College. I have been most fortunate in having had, over several years, many colleagues and research students who have contributed greatly to the ideas and to the hard work that go toward the slow—the enormously slow—unravelling of some of the problems that we tackled. Without their collaboration in research, many of the facts I cite would not have been known. But this does not mean that any one of them has to accept the responsibility for the arguments I have used in this book or in the conclusions that I draw; this responsibility is mine alone.

The arguments and conclusions are certainly not complete or final. Whatever we or others have discovered in relation to the problems I discuss is far less than what remains to be discovered. But it is now clear to me, as I hope it will soon be clear to you, that there is already very good reason for us to consider sugar a highly dangerous food—and to act accordingly.

Finally, I feel I must say here how grateful I am to the many firms in the food and pharmaceutical industries that for twenty-five years have given me such constant and generous support in the building up and maintenance of the department of nutrition. For many of them, the results of our research were often not at all in their interests; yet it was largely with their help that we were able to work on those problems that, to me, seemed of such importance.

John Yudkin, M.D.

Queen Elizabeth College
London University
1972

1

What's So Different About Sugar?

Sugar is common enough in all our lives, and almost everyone believes that it is simply an attractive sweet—one of many carbohydrates in the diet of civilized countries. But sugar is really quite an extraordinary substance. It is unique in the plant that makes it, in the materials that chemists can produce from it, and in its use in foods at home and in industry. And research is only now beginning to show that it also has unique effects in the body, different from those of other carbohydrates. Since it now amounts to about one-fifth of the total calories consumed in the wealthier countries, it is essential that everyone know more about what it does to people when it enters the body in food and drink.

Curiously enough, not only the layman but also the physician and the medical research worker have until recently assumed that there was no need to bother with any special study of sugar. Since man began to produce his food instead of hunting and gathering it, his diet has contained large amounts of carbohydrates. It did not seem to occur to anyone that it made any difference

3

whether this carbohydrate derived almost entirely from starch in wheat or rice or maize, or whether the starch was gradually becoming replaced by increasing amounts of sugar, as has been happening in the last 100 or 200 years.

Although some early research workers occasionally pointed out that eating sugar was not always the same as eating starch, no one paid much attention to this until ten years or so ago. When I wrote a book on weight reduction in 1958, I strongly recommended a diet low in carbohydrate, but I made very little distinction between the benefits of avoiding starch and the benefits of avoiding sugar. Since that time, an enormous amount of new information has been accumulating, and more is being added constantly. Most of the new research has, quite properly, appeared in scientific and medical journals, but it seems now high time to summarize it for nontechnical people, especially mothers and housewives. After all, it is not only scientists and physicians who eat, and if eating sugar really is dangerous, then everyone should be told about it.

The fact that so much about the effects of sugar is still being discovered is in itself an illustration of how different these effects are from those of other common foods. You might have imagined that the realization that there were differences would have stimulated the sugar producers and refiners themselves to initiate studies into the properties of their product. Other industries that produce foods like meat or dairy products or fruits have spent a great deal of money over the years to carry out or support nutritional studies on their products, even though these foods form a much smaller proportion of the Western diet than sugar now does. But the sugar people seem quite content to spend their money on advertising and public relations, making claims about quick energy, and simply rejecting suggestions that sugar is really harmful to the heart or the teeth or the figure or to health in general.

I cannot claim that everything I say in this book will be accepted by every research worker. I hope, however, that I have made it clear which parts of the book refer to solid, observable scientific research and which parts are my own opinions and interpretations of these observations. Only time will show how right or how wrong I am in any one particular personal statement.

But right at the outset I can make two key statements that no one can refute:

First, *there is no physiological requirement for sugar;* all human nutritional needs can be met in full without having to take a single spoon of white or brown or raw sugar, on its own or in any food or drink.

Secondly, *if only a small fraction of what is already known about the effects of sugar were to be revealed in relation to any other material used as a food additive, that material would promptly be banned.*

Think of what happened to cyclamate. Many countries now do not permit this sugar substitute to be used, and the prohibition is based on experiments in which rats were fed for an enormously long time on huge amounts of cyclamate—the equivalent of a man consuming ten to twelve pounds of sugar every day for forty or fifty years. Later in these pages you can read what can happen to rats fed sugar in amounts not very (if at all) different from those taken by quite a lot of people. I will not anticipate the details that you will find, but the very many effects include enlarged and fatty livers, enlarged kidneys, and a shortening of life span.

Think of all this the next time you read of an experiment suggesting that another sugar substitute, saccharine, may be harmful; and the blaze of publicity encouraged by the busy men and women who run such organizations as Sugar Information, Inc., or the British Sugar Bureau. Then think of what is already known that sugar *can* do, as distinct from what cyclamate or saccharine might *possibly* do if taken in enormously unrealistic amounts for a long enough time.

Let me add a word here about these two sugar substitutes, saccharine and cyclamate. First, they are two quite different materials, although both are made in the laboratory; they do not exist in nature. Secondly, they have the property of being exceedingly sweet; cyclamate is about 30 times as sweet as sugar and saccharine about 550 times as sweet. Because of this, a very small amount of cyclamate or an almost invisibly tiny amount of saccharine is as sweet as one teaspoon of sugar.

Thirdly, saccharine has two slight disadvantages over cyclamate. For some people it leaves a bitter aftertaste; and it cannot be used for canned or other foods or drinks that have to be heated, because it decomposes which makes for an unpleasant smell and taste. Fourthly, they are not effective sugar substitutes in some foods, such as candy, chocolate and ice cream, because sugar is needed in these to produce other qualities, such as bulkiness.

My own view is that it is perfectly safe to use these sweeteners whenever you wish to, although (for what I consider quite inadequate reasons) you cannot find cyclamate in some countries. But even though they are quite safe, some people think it a good idea not to use them. They prefer to get into the habit of having less sweetness in their foods and drinks by avoiding those which, as I have just said, *must* be made with sugar.

Many people have criticized what I have previously written; they say that the experiments that we and others have carried out have used absurdly high amounts of sugar to produce the effects we describe. One such person is the American physiologist Dr. Ancel Keys, the most important and certainly the most dogmatic research worker expounding the view that coronary disease comes from dietary fat and that sugar has nothing whatever to do with it. He has written that "the levels of sugar in the experimental diets are of the order of three or more times that in any natural diet." This is quite untrue, as we shall see, but it comes about because very few people have bothered to find out how much sugar people do, in fact, consume.

You hear stories that the Turks take a very great deal of sugar, as you can see from the amounts they put into their coffee. But the Turks even now only take about one-third of the amount consumed in Britain and in the United States, and ten years ago the Turks took less than one-quarter. Apart from questions like these, you can also go wrong when you look at official statistics without reading the small print. There have been regular annual reports of the British diet for the last thirty years, and the figures given for sugar amount to an average of about sixty pounds a year. But if you look carefully, you will see that the statistics do not include snacks or food eaten away from home, and the real average turns out to be nearly twice as much, 120 pounds of sugar a year. If you now take into account that this is an average and that many people take much more sugar than the average, you will find that the quantities used in experiments in man and in animals are by no means extraordinary or absurd.

And what about Dr. Keys' reference to the sugar content of "any natural diet"? What *is* a natural diet? Is it natural for Westerners today to eat twenty times as much sugar, or more, than our ancestors ate only two or three hundred years ago? Nowadays one so often hears the words "natural" and "moderate"; one really must be on one's guard not to be misled into believing that they have any real meaning; or, even worse, that they provide evidence that something to which these words are applied is intrinsically wholesome, good, and desirable.

I hope that when you have finished this book I shall have convinced you that sugar is really dangerous. At the very least, I hope I shall have persuaded you that it *might* be dangerous. Now add to this the fact, the indubitable fact, that neither you nor your children need to take any added sugar at all, or foods or drinks made with it, in order to enjoy a completely healthy and highly nutritious diet. If, as a result, you give up all or most of your sugar-eating—and I shall show you that this is not too difficult—I shall not have wasted my time in writing this book; more important, you will not have wasted your time reading it.

2

Everybody Likes the Sweet

One of the most spectacular current "growth industries" is that concerned with the production and distribution of health foods. In Britain and the United States almost every neighborhood has its special store where you can, it seems, ensure eternal youth by buying hand-woven honey, free-range carrots, and stone-ground eggs.

There is no doubt that people today are very worried about their food. But different people are worried about different things, and most of them are worried about the wrong things. I can assure you that it really does not matter to your health whether your chicken is produced by the broiler system, or whether you eat potatoes grown with chemical fertilizers, or whether your bread is white or brown. But it *does* matter that your diet is now very likely to be different from what evolved over millions of years as the diet most suitable for you as a member of the species *Homo sapiens*.

Please don't take these sentences to imply that I have discovered the secrets of the ideal diet. Because I have written rather teasingly about "natural foods," I do not mean to imply that everything you see in the health-food store is nonsense and that everything I shall be telling you is an absolute certainty. It is true, though, that every person tends to believe that a knowledge of nutrition is somehow instinctive and that careful thought and introspection will provide as good an answer to nutritional questions as do the studies and research of the professional nutritionist.

It is silly to insist, in spite of all the detailed evidence to the contrary, that there are any differences in the nutritional value of potatoes produced on land fertilized by chemical fertilizers and those fertilized by compost. On the other hand, it is equally silly of some researchers to imagine that science knows all there is to know about human nutrition. There is, for example, no justification for the statement I heard at a recent scientific meeting, where a food chemist said that scientists don't have to concern themselves too much about producing enough high protein foods; man shall soon be able to feed himself entirely with synthetic protein and other nutrients. And this at a time when new facts are discovered almost daily about such supposedly well-understood phenomena as obesity; or about the effects of different dietary carbohydrates. The safest position is somewhere between arrogance based on un-recognized ignorance, and arrogance based on un-warranted certainty.

But how does one find this position? What principles does one best adopt to decide whether this or that food is "good for you"? What indeed should the ideal diet be?

I am going to devote the rest of this chapter to trying to answer these questions, slowly and carefully, because I believe that an understanding of the biology of the diet provides the clues to what the Western diet should be; what is wrong with it today; and why it has gone wrong.

You might remind yourself that all animals require two sorts of materials for their growth and survival. One is material that can be burned (oxidized) to yield the energy needed for the processes of living—growth and movement and breathing, and all the other activities that distinguish a living animal from a dead one. These materials for energy production are mainly carbohydrates and fats, although protein can also be used. The second sort of materials consists of those thousands of different compounds that go to make up the very complex chemical composition of the cells of the different tissues that in turn constitute the whole living animal.

Now, the vast majority of these compounds can be made by the body itself, from a very much smaller number of raw materials. But these are all materials that must, each one of them, be supplied to the body. Without them, a young organism cannot grow, and an adult organism will gradually waste away because it is unable to make good the general wear and tear of its cells and tissues.

So one can say at this point that the body has to be given materials that go both to supply energy and to provide the raw materials for growth and repair. The source of these essential materials is our food and drink. These have to supply about fifty different items. They fall into several classes—the carbohydrates, the fats, the proteins, the vitamins, the mineral elements, and, of course, water.

As far as science knows, every single species of animal needs the same components for life and sustenance. And almost every single species has to get all of these out of food. The exceptions are interesting, and include ruminants, like the cow, which can get many vitamins from microbes living in their complicated stomachs. But in general, as I said, most animals have to get all of their vitamins, protein, etc., from their food, and they need these nutrients in roughly the same proportions in their diets.

You could therefore argue that all species of animals should be choosing to eat the same foods. But in fact it is well known that different species eat very different diets indeed. Some, like the lion and the tiger, are largely carnivorous—meat-eating. Others, like rabbits and giraffes and deer, are largely herbivorous—plant-eating, or vegetarian. Others again, like man and the rat and the pig, eat diets that come from both animal and plant sources; these animals are omnivorous. By contrast, some animals eat from only a very limited range of foods; the giraffe eats little except leaves from acacia trees. The koala bear eats little except eucalyptus leaves, and then only from a few of the eighty or so species found in Australia.

So there exists an apparent contradiction. First, all species of animals require the same in the way of nutrients, which—with a few exceptions—they must get from their food. But secondly, different species of animals get these same nutrients from very different sorts of diet. Great biological advantages flow from this, because it prevents the various species' competing with one another for the same foods. Each species establishes its own "ecological niche" in regard to its food supply. Its anatomy and physiology are well adapted to find, acquire, eat, chew, and digest the foods that it chooses.

But the fact remains that one species will often not even attempt to eat foods that are highly sought after by another species. So, what makes one animal choose one sort of diet, and a different animal choose a completely different sort? Clearly, it cannot be that they are choosing these different foods for the nutrients they contain, since their nutrient needs are so similar. It must therefore be some other properties of foods that make one range of foods look especially attractive to one species, and another range especially attractive to another. These qualities are shape and size, color and smell, taste and texture—features that I'd like to lump together, perhaps too loosely, under the heading of "palatability."

Foods, then, possess two different properties—palatability and nutritional value. The palatability of foods, and so the foods chosen to make up the total diet, varies from species to species; however, the nutritional needs that have to be satisfied by these various species are virtually the same for all species. Thus, animals choose diets that they find palatable, but whatever these diets are, they must supply all their nutritional needs. If they did not, the animals would perish.

So one can say that when an animal eats what it wants, it gets what it needs; or, in the terms I have just been using, for each sort of animal, palatability is a guide to nutritional value. Everyone instinctively feels that this is correct; if you like some food very much it is taken to indicate—to prove, almost—that you need this food.

Eating habits are formed in childhood, and children like sweet foods. Does it follow that sugar must be food for them? Not at all, although I am sure that most people have heard this sort of argument. One also hears phrases like the one in the old music-hall song, "A little of what you fancy does you good." And so long as man did not manufacture foods, this argument was perfectly sound.

THE ORIGIN OF MAN'S DIET

I shall come back later to the question of when it is true that what you want is what you need, and when it is not true. Let me now pick up the story of palatability and nutritional value, and see how it applies to our own species.

Science is gradually learning quite a lot about man's origin, and although there are still a lot of uncertainties about his diet, one can now make some pretty good guesses. It is generally agreed that man's earliest ancestors, the squirrel-like primate of some 70 million years ago, were vegetarian. They continued as vegetarians up to and after the emergence of Proconsul about 20 million years ago, for they had no difficulty in surviving on fruits, nuts, berries, and leaves. But then the rainfall began to decrease, and the earth entered a 12-million-year period of drought. The forests shrank and their place was taken by the ever-increasing areas of open savannah. It was during this time that *Australopithecus gracilis* emerged.

The survival of this Southern man-ape depended on his forsaking the vegetarian and fruitarian existence of his brother man-ape, *Australopithecus robustus,* and changing to a predatory and hunting existence that was largely carnivorous. The molar teeth of *gracilis* had the shape and thin enamel of a carnivore. His jaw muscles were small and did not need the crested cranium of *robustus* for their attachment. His canines were also small, for he killed neither with fangs nor with claws or horns, but with weapons. This he could do since he had adopted a completely erect posture, and his arms and hands were freed from the need to be used for locomotion. His earliest weapons were bones; only later did he begin to use stones and still later the axe.

Thus it appears that for several million years man's ancestors were largely meat-eating. From that time, man and his immediate ancestors continued to be hunters and predators and scavengers, seeking their favorite food of meat and offal.

They had one advantage over the more strictly carnivorous species in that they could, and did, eat vegetable foods, too. Along with meat, their diets occasionally contained the nuts, berries, leaves, and roots that fed their forebears. This omnivorous potential gave them the ability to survive when their prey eluded them or was scarce.

In nutritional terms, the diet of prehistoric man and his ancestors during perhaps 2 million years or more was rich in protein, moderately rich in fat, and usually poor in carbohydrate. If one may assume that man's present universal taste preferences for the sweet and meaty are a continuation of preferences acquired long ago, then it is likely that, except in times of hunger, the small amounts of dietary carbohydrate will have come mostly from fruits, as opposed to the less palatable leaves and roots. This would imply that the (digestible) carbohydrate consisted mostly of sugars and relatively little starch.

THE TWO FOOD REVOLUTIONS

Until very recently (in evolutionary terms), all animals, including man, depended for their food supplies on hunting or scavenging other animals, or the consumption of wild vegetation. It was less than 10,000 years ago—compared with the 2 million years or more of his carnivorous ancestry—that man became, uniquely, a food producer. He discovered that some of the wild grasses from which he occasionally ate the seeds could yield many times that amount of edible seed if they were deliberately planted The domestication of these grasses became the cereals that are now the staple food of a large part of present-day mankind, and it was followed, or accompanied, by the domestication of root crops and of wild animals that were used, not only as animals of burden, but for food.

The results of the discovery of agriculture—the Neolithic revolution—were many and far-reaching. Man ceased being a nomad and began to live in settled, socially organized communities. This landmark of progress became the basis for all we know of civilization, with its arts, its inventions, and its discoveries.

Compared with hunting and foraging, agriculture usually yielded more food; it also allowed man to cultivate areas where existing resources of food would have been inadequate. Thus the human population grew, because fewer died of food shortage and because man spread into increasing areas of the earth's surface. But in due course the limits of food production again became the limits to the numbers that could be fed. The inevitable pressure of population on food supplies tended to produce and stabilize a type of diet quite different from that of man's hunting ancestors. It was—and still is—much easier to produce vegetable foods than animal foods; for a given area of land, some ten times as many calories can be produced in the form of cereals or root crops than in the form of meat, eggs, or milk.

The effect of the Neolithic revolution was thus to alter the components of the diet so that it was now rich in carbohydrate and poor both in protein and in fat.

The carbohydrate was overwhelmingly starch, with sugars supplied only to a small extent, as before, by wild fruits. It is likely that both protein deficiency and deficiency of many of the vitamins began to affect large sections of the human species only after man became a food producer.

Man, like all animals, constantly faces recurring periods of food shortage. Although the Neolithic revolution increased total food supplies for mankind and radically changed the composition of his diet, hunger and famine did not vanish. For most of the time, wind, drought, flood, and man's own exploitation of the land have combined to limit food production to levels lower than those necessary to feed all his offspring. It is only in the last few decades that a sizable proportion of mankind—though still only a minority—has been born into a situation where it is unlikely that real hunger will ever be experienced throughout a lifetime.

The reasons for this second revolutionary change are the cumulative effects of science and technology. I need only list a few of these to show the extent of this revolution and its effect upon the availability of food to mankind: genetics and the breeding of improved varieties of plants and animals for food; engineering and its effect on drainage and irrigation; the discovery of synthetic fertilizers, weed killers, and pesticides; the internal combustion engine and its effect upon transport by sea, land, and air; modern methods of food preservation by canning, dehydration, deep freezing; and I could cite many more examples of changes that have given man the possibility of producing and preserving much more food than has ever been available to any other species.

As a result, a large proportion of the populations in the affluent countries has a very wide choice of foods, irrespective of season or geography. The effect has been that these peoples are able more and more to choose foods that please their palates, and not simply foods that fill their stomachs. The first and most obvious result has been an increase in the consumption of more palatable foods such as meat and fruit. And because of the basic association between palatability and nutrition, there has come a simultaneous improvement in the nutritional standards in these groups, just as there has always been a better level of nutrition in the much smaller section that comprised the wealthy members of any population.

The advances in agricultural techniques and general technology have had an effect not only on the yield of food and the availability of food. They have also had a tremendous effect on the way foods can be deliberately changed by extractions and additions, so that quite new manufactured foods can be made that do not exist in anything like these forms in nature. Some of these manufactured foods have been in existence for quite a long time—bread for example, and tortillas and chappatis and cakes, cookies, and biscuits. But most of them have been produced, or vastly improved, only in the past century or two or in recent decades. I am thinking now of ice cream and soft drinks, an enormous range of chocolate and candy, and new sorts of sweet snacks and cookies. And soon there is to be a new range of "meat" products made from textured vegetable or microbial protein.

We can do all these things largely because nutritional value and palatability are two different qualities. As I pointed out, although man can use as food almost any sort of animal or vegetable material, his preferences are for the particular palatability qualities of meat and of fruit, which together can supply all the nutrients he requires. Researchers are only just beginning to emulate the taste and texture of meat; and people will be eating and relishing the new vegetable or microbial protein foods only when the food manufacturer imparts to them qualities that make them much more attractive than he has been able to make them—up to now. But for some time industry has been able to isolate an essence of sweetness, which has the property of imparting a very desirable palatability to a wide range of foods and drinks. People do not demand a particular flavor and texture to go with sweetness, although they seem to demand at least a very limited range of flavors and textures to go with meaty and salty foods.

Man's avidity for sweetness could for vast periods of time be satisfied almost exclusively by the eating of fruit; rarely, and in very small quantities, he was lucky enough to find some honey produced by wild bees. But some time after the Neolithic revolution, perhaps only 2,500 years ago, he found that he could produce a crude sort of sugar by extracting and drying the sap of the sugar cane. This he first began to cultivate probably in India, and its cultivation slowly spread to China, Arabia, the Mediterranean, and later to South and West Africa, the Canary Islands, Brazil, and the Caribbean.

In spite of this increasing area of cultivation, the cost of the sugar, crude as it was, was extremely high, so that by the middle of the sixteenth century it was said to be equivalent to the present cost of caviar. Compared with the price of foods such as butter or eggs, it has been calculated that the price of sugar has fallen to about one two-hundredth of its price in the fifteenth century. Even as late as the eighteenth century, sugar was a luxury, and domestic sugar boxes until one hundred years or so ago were often provided with lock and key.

It was chiefly the development of the sugar plantations in the Caribbean, based on the slave trade, that set the pattern of the sugar industry in the form known today. The demand for sugar was so great, and its production so lucrative, that from about the middle of the eighteenth century tremendous improvements began to be made in the production of high-yielding sugar cane (and later the sugar beet); in the efficiency of the extraction of the sugar and the making of raw sugar; and finally in the process of refining the sugar. Consequently, the price fell constantly, the demand grew, and consumption rose to exceedingly high levels.

Legislators in many countries have often taxed sugar to provide revenue, just as they have often taxed tobacco and alcohol. And sugar also resembles alcohol and tobacco in that it is a material for which people rapidly develop a craving, and for which there is nevertheless no physiological need.

I am saying, then, that man has a natural liking for sweet things; that primitive man could satisfy this desire by eating fruit, or to a much lesser extent by eating honey; and that in eating fruit because he liked it, he obtained nutrients (such as vitamin C) that he needs. But now he can satisfy the desire for sweetness by consuming foods or drinks that provide little or no nutritional value except calories. It is possible today to get an orange drink that is more attractive in color than true orange juice, is sweeter in taste, has a more aromatic flavor, is cheaper to buy—and can be guaranteed to contain no vitamin C whatever.

Since people chiefly seek palatability in foods and drinks, the sale of these drinks increases all the time. One day it will no doubt be possible to manufacture from some nondigestible polymer a hamburger that looks more attractive than a real meat hamburger, smells and sizzles better on the barbeque, and at only half the price. It will be entirely "pure" in that it will contain neither protein nor vitamins nor minerals. And who will say that people shall not buy this super, space-age new food just because it has no nutritional value? People shall buy it because they like it, and only because they like it.

Most people still believe that foods that are palatable must *ipso facto* also have a high nutritional value; many also believe what is equally untrue—that foods with little flavor have no nutritional value. I am certain that it is the dissociation of palatability and nutritional value that is the major cause of the "malnutrition of affluence." For this reason, let me give you one or two more examples of how one can no longer expect the two qualities to be found necessarily together.

First, you may remember beef tea, which even in this century was commonly given by doctors to their convalescent patients as a "restorative." And to this day many mothers believe that a tasty clear soup is nourishing for their children. Yet here is high palatability with virtually no nutritional value. Secondly, the economics of chicken farming has produced a broiler chicken which, because it is slaughtered young, and because of the speed with which it is eviscerated, has less flavor than a free-range chicken. Yet its nutritional value is no different, even though its lower palatability is often referred to as indicating a lower nutritional value.

A little while ago I read a short story the title and author of which I have unfortunately forgotten. A brilliant chemist became tired of his mistress and decided to get rid of her by using his professional skill. He devoted himself to developing a new and exquisite flavor, which he then incorporated into chocolates, and he sent box after box to his mistress. Finding these quite irresistible, she consumed them in inordinate quantities until she died of over-eating. The chemist knew that her craving would alone suffice to kill her.

One more example of the strong power of palatability is the snake that ordinarily will eat only toads. It will not, for example, eat pieces of such meat as beef. But you can make it do so by rubbing the beef onto the skin of the toad, so presumably making the beef taste of toad.

A major argument used by the health-food people to demonstrate the poor nutritional value of modern processed foods is that they have little flavor. Their own products, they say, *must* be nutritionally superior because they taste better. Much of what I have to say in this book is based on the proposition that satisfying one's palate is no longer a guarantee that one is satisfying nutritional needs.

3

What Sugar Is—
and Isn't

It is very confusing when people use different words for the same thing. In England, we say "lift" for what you Americans call "elevator," "property" when you say "real estate," and "petrol" when you say "gas." But even greater misunderstandings arise when people use the same word for different things. The American woman carries a handbag, which she sometimes calls her purse, while an English woman carries a handbag in which she has a much smaller purse for her money. The American woman carries her money in her wallet.

THERE IS SUGAR—AND THEN THERE IS SUGAR

Sugar sometimes means the beautiful white powder or lumps that this book is all about, but sometimes it means a different substance that circulates in the blood. Another example is the word "energy," which, as I shall discuss, means one thing to a layman and quite another thing to the nutritionist.

Chemists apply the word "sugar" to any one of a group of substances that have similar properties but are not identical. Some of the better-known sugars are glucose, fructose, maltose, lactose, and sucrose. They have other names as well; fructose is fruit sugar, lactose is milk sugar, maltose is malt sugar, and sucrose is the ordinary familiar table sugar that you use in tea and coffee, and for making cakes, cookies, ice cream, and soft drinks.

Glucose is a sugar that is found, usually with other sugars, in some fruits and vegetables. It is very important to biochemists, physiologists, and nutritionists because it is a key material in the metabolism of all plants and animals. Many of man's principal foods are sooner or later converted into glucose, and glucose forms one of the most important substances that is metabolized or oxidized or burned in the tissues to give everybody energy for everyday activities.

There is always glucose in the blood stream, and this is usually called "blood sugar." In healthy people, a complicated interaction of a number of hormones contrives to keep the level of the blood sugar fairly constant. If you eat something like ordinary sugar or starch in your food, glucose will be released during digestion, and this will be absorbed from the alimentary canal into the blood. The level of blood glucose therefore rises. Immediately, however, there is an outflow of hormones, especially insulin from the pancreas; the effect of this is to lower the level of glucose toward its normal level. This works chiefly by converting it into a substance called glycogen and tucking this away in the muscles and liver where it can be called upon again to release glucose if the level in the blood falls.

Almost every book written by people in, or associated with, the sugar industry contains a section where you are told how important sugar is because it is an essential component of the body. It is oxidized so as to give energy, it is a key material in all sorts of metabolic processes, and so on. And they imply, or even say explicitly, that all this applies to "sugar" (sucrose). In fact, they have been talking about "blood sugar" (glucose).

Glucose and sucrose are by no means identical. They have different chemical structures, and there are important ways in which they have different effects in the body. When the word "sugar" is used in such a way that at one moment it means the sucrose in your food, and at another moment the glucose in your blood, these differences in their effects—crucial, as we shall see—are hidden. So accustomed do people become to this case of mistaken identity that they eventually find it difficult to accept that the sucrose they eat and the glucose in the blood may be different in quite vital ways.

WHERE ENERGY COMES FROM

"Sugar works for you with each bite you eat—for your body is an energy factory with sugar as its fuel." This is a quotation from a pamphlet issued by a sugar firm. But what does "energy" really mean?

When you say, "I have no energy," or "Little Johnny is full of energy," you use "energy" to mean either physical activity or the inclination to be physically active. When you say that Johnny is full of energy, you picture him rushing around, leaping up and down stairs, climbing a tree, or tearing along on his bicycle. On the other hand, when you say you have no energy, you imply that you do not want to do anything much other than sit about, or preferably lie down.

So when someone says, "Sugar gives you energy," you imagine that this is just what you need to leap out of your chair and dash around just like little Johnny. But the physiologist and the nutritionist who talk about sugar and energy mean something different. What they mean is that sugar (like any other food, incidentally) can be utilized by the body to release the energy you need for all the functions of the body. These include such automatic activities as breathing or heart-beating or digestion, and all the chemical reactions called metabolism. They also include such voluntary activities as dressing or shaving or walking or running.

What people really mean when they say that sugar gives them energy is simply that it is a potential source of the energy needed for the processes of living. It is there when you need it, in the same way as the gas (or petrol) that you put into your car is in the tank, ready to be burned when you want the car engine to go. Just putting another gallon or two in the tank does not, of itself, make the car go any faster, or make it any more energetic. And taking another spoonful of sugar does not, of itself, make you jump out of your chair and rush to mow the lawn.

All food, then, contains "energy" in that some of its components can provide the fuel for the body's workings. Normally you have quite a sizable reserve of this fuel in your tissues, stored from the food you have eaten on previous occasions. If you were starving, so that you had little or none of these reserves, and if in addition it were imperative that you have some fuel in your tissues within minutes, in addition to the glucose in your blood, then it might be a good idea to eat sugar rather than any other food, because the sugar quickly gets digested and absorbed and taken to the tissues. A piece of bread and butter would take a few minutes longer.

This insignificant time differential is what the sugar propagandists mean when they talk about sugar's "quick" energy. But isn't it really quite rare for circumstances to arise that make it important for you to take advantage of this more rapid availability of "energy" from sugar? And besides, as we shall see later, it may be that the rapidity with which sugar floods the blood stream is harmful rather than beneficial.

I sometimes wonder whether the insistence that sugar contains energy arises from the fact that it contains nothing else. All other foods contain energy as well as at least *some* nutrients in the way of protein or minerals or vitamins or a mixture of these. Sugar contains energy, and that is all.

IS "PURE" GOOD?

As I have shown, the combination of all foods contains the whole range of essential materials that the body needs for its survival and well-being. Each one of these is derived from living plants or living animals; if they are not processed in any way, they contain a mixture of the approximately fifty essential materials. From a cabbage, you obtain, among other essentials, some vitamin A and vitamin C and calcium. From a piece of meat you obtain protein, fat, several vitamins of the B group, iron, and many other nutrients.

But suppose one were to cultivate pine trees instead

of cabbages, and then extract the vitamin C and eat that instead of eating cabbages? It would be possible now to claim that you have consumed absolutely pure vitamin C, but it would not be of any particular advantage to get it this way rather than from the cabbage. In fact, you would lose out in this transaction because the cabbage would have given you other nutritional benefits apart from vitamin C.

Yet this is really the sort of thing that people do when they make sugar. They plant vast areas of land with sugar cane or sugar beet instead of crops that they can eat more or less whole. Then they take the cane or beat and extract, clean, filter, refine, and purify it until they have something that is virtually 100 percent sugar. At this point, the refiners say with absolute truth that this sugar is one of the purest foods known.

Once more a word is being used in two different senses. When you say water is pure, or bread, or butter, you mean that it is not contaminated with anything inferior, and especially not contaminated with anything harmful. But then you are persuaded to carry over this sense of wholesomeness to the chemists' meaning: a material that does not have something else mixed with it, irrespective of whether this something would have been harmful or harmless or even beneficial.

There is no special reason to praise sugar for the fact that, in the course of its elaborate preparation, it is freed from all other materials so that it is chemically "pure," as are most of the other materials the chemist has on his laboratory shelves. Equally, I would see no reason for being pleased at being presented with pure protein for my consumption, or pure vitamin B_{12}, or any other dietary component in its isolated state. What virtue would this represent?

IS "REFINED" BAD?

By now I am pretty sure I have the warm support of those who think that it is refined sugar we should avoid and that none of my strictures apply to the raw and brown sugars. I must now ask you to bear with me while I explain two apparently contradictory things. First, degrees of refining make virtually no difference to the harmfulness of sugar. Secondly, you will be much healthier if you use only brown sugar and never eat any food with refined sugar.

To explain this apparent paradox, it is useful to look very briefly at the essentials of a most elaborate and highly efficient process, the manufacture of sugar from the sugar cane.

The tall canes are cut by machetes or by mechanical harvesters, loaded onto trucks, and taken to the factory. They are there chopped into small pieces that move through crushing rollers. Then they are sprayed with water and the juice is squeezed out. The juice contains something like 12 or 13 percent sugar, but in addition some 3 percent of extraneous matter.

It is now filtered and passed into heating vessels, and lime is added. The effect of this treatment is to coagulate and separate a great deal of the unwanted material. The mixture is poured into tanks where this solid matter settles so that the clarified juice can be poured off into evaporators. When the juice is concentrated sufficiently, it is poured into vacuum pans, so that the concentration of the juice can be continued at lower temperatures in order to avoid caramelizing the sugar unduly.

Eventually, the sugar begins to crystallize, and becomes a "massecuite"—a mixture of sugar crystals and syrup. These are separated by spinning the massecuite in a centrifuge at up to 1,200 revolutions per minute. The result is two products—raw sugar and cane molasses (or syrup). The molasses is boiled twice more, and the process of crystallization and centrifugation is repeated. After this, there is usually not enough sugar left in the molasses to make it worthwhile to continue the process. Nevertheless, the final molasses still contains a little sugar, and it is used in a variety of ways, for example, to make rum or yeast or cattle food.

The raw sugar contains about 96 percent sucrose, rather more than 1 percent water, and about 3 percent unwanted other matter. During the process of refining, almost every trace of the water and of the extraneous substances is removed so that the final product is over 99.9 percent pure sucrose. The purification is done by washing and filtering the raw sugar, decolorizing it by passing it over charcoal, and then crystallizing and drying the final product. The washing and filtering are necessary because raw sugar is quite dirty; it contains particles of sand and earth, molds, bacteria, and perhaps sugar lice.

Sugar from the sugar beet is produced in much the same way. There are only one or two important differences. One is that the process goes right through from the beet to the refined sugar, since the beet is actually grown in those countries (like the United States and Britain) where the refining processes normally take place. Another difference is that beet molasses, unlike cane sugar molasses, are not used for human consumption since they are quite unpalatably bitter. A third difference is that the beet, unlike the cane, is not crushed, but the juice is allowed to diffuse out from cut-up pieces of beet. From then onward, the preparation of raw beet sugar and its refining resemble the process for cane sugar. The final product, beet sugar, is identical to cane sugar—not rather like, not even very similar, but identical.

Although some people like brown sugar at least for some purposes, the majority have always demanded that their sugar be as white as possible. One hundred years ago and more, the sugar that was bought by the housewife came in cones and was not quite white. She would herself then often wash it to improve its appearance. And the manufacturers helped to cover up the yellowish off-white color by packing the sugar cones, and later the cubes or crystals, in blue bags. In the same way, the white laundry used to be finished off by a final rinse with "laundry blue," nowadays usually replaced by fluorescent additives that produce a similar effect.

Obviously it would not be very wise to eat raw cane sugar, since, as I showed, it is dirty. On the other hand, there are some brown sugars that not only are clean and edible but have attractive caramel-like flavors. This is because they contain some of the molasses that have not been entirely removed during refining. Some of the brown sugars are made in the countries where the sugar is grown, and are produced simply by cutting short the refining process so that the sugar retains some of the colored syrupy molasses that are otherwise washed away or removed by the final refining treatment. Sometimes they are made by refining sugar until it consists of the usual pure white crystals, and then adding a little brown caramel.

Against this background it is finally possible to look at the question about the nutritional effects of refining foods.

"Brown Is Beautiful"

4

"Brown Is Beautiful"

Among the causes that have been suggested for some of the diseases of affluence, one that is commonly put forward is the over-consumption of "refined carbohydrate"—meaning white sugar and white bread. There are often several very good reasons for implicating sugar, but there is little reason for implicating bread.

Let me first deal with the question of the lowering of the nutritional value of these foods by the refining process. The common assumption is that brown sugar and brown bread are excellent foods and rich in nourishment, especially because they contain vitamins and mineral elements. White sugar and white bread, on the other hand, are supposed to be devoid of nourishment; or, at any rate, they are supposed to contain no useful quantities of nutrients.

I shall soon show that none of the brown sugars contains any worthwhile amounts of nutrients and that they do not contribute seriously to the quantities of vitamins or minerals that the body needs. Even raw sugar, which is not refined at all, cannot be considered a source of nutrients, even if one assumes that anyone might really want to eat this dirty material.

Suppose you did eat one or another of the brown sugars, such as Barbados sugar. Suppose you used no other sugar all day. This would imply, incidentally, that you could not eat the majority of manufactured foods and drinks that you can buy in most shops, and you would have a rather peculiar taste if you put it in your tea. But you might nevertheless, if you tried hard, get through two ounces a day. Let me exaggerate and say you would take as much as three and one-half ounces a day (100 grams). This would give you around 400 calories, about one-sixth or one-seventh of your daily caloric needs. But it would give you only about one-sixtieth of your needs of vitamin B_1 and of riboflavin (vitamin B_2). It would give you no iron or calcium or anything else of value.

Now let me do the same calculation for raw sugar, except that I really must be more realistic and say that it is difficult to imagine that you could take more than one ounce of this a day. You would then get much less of the vitamins B_1 and B_2: about one two-hundredths of your needs of B_1 and one-hundredth of B_2. You would also get one-fiftieth of your daily needs of calcium. The only nutrient in any quantity is iron, but even so, one ounce of raw sugar supplies only one-twentieth of what you need for the day. The iron, by the way, comes mostly from the tiny quantities worn off the machinery in which the sugar is prepared from the cane.

One of the best ways to get misled about foods and their nutritive value is to forget that you not only need nutrients but need each of them in sufficient amounts. People seem to be quite impressed if they are told that pickled melon seeds (or whatever) contain vitamins

A and B and C, and a lot of different mineral elements. This is about as sensible as saying that a man is wealthy because he has money, without bothering to ask how much money. If you tell me I can get half the vitamin B_1 I need for a day from five pounds of raw sugar or from five slices of bread, I know which I would consider the more sensible source.

The situation with bread is different, and in two ways. First, brown bread, unlike brown sugar, can contribute substantial amounts of nutrients to your diet. Secondly, white bread can contribute almost as much, and it is quite wrong to think that it contains "nothing but starch." You can say that brown sugar is as bad as white sugar, but it is also true that white bread is in most ways as good as brown bread.

I had better start by pointing out that there are lots of different sorts of brown bread. The brownest would be made from flour in which the whole of the wheat is used, including the bran. This would be called 100 percent extraction. Because of the bran, it is too gritty for most people, so not very much of this bread is eaten. In Britain, it is common for the bran to be removed, leaving about 92 percent extraction of flour, and this is used to make what is known as wholewheat bread. Most people in Britain and the United States eat white bread, and this is made up of flour of about 72 percent extraction. The 28 percent that is removed by milling contains chiefly the germ as well as the bran.

In addition, there are several other sorts of bread, some made by separating the various parts of the wheat grain and then mixing some of the fractions in different proportions.

It is wrong to suppose that in white bread all that is left is pure starch. For example, white flour contains only fractionally less protein than does brown flour—

about 13 percent instead of about 13.5 percent. And in many countries, such as the United States and the United Kingdom, some of the vitamins that are partly removed with the milling are replaced by the flour millers. Moreover, other nutrients are sometimes added to a much higher level than was present in the original wheat grain—calcium, for example, in Britain.

There is one other difference between white bread and wholewheat bread. This is the amount of cellulose or fiber: white bread contains very little; wholewheat bread about 1.5 percent. For this reason, wholewheat bread tends to have a slightly laxative effect.

It is just about possible to imagine that people might suffer from a nutritional deficiency if they were eating the standard fortified white bread instead of good, high extraction brown bread. You would have to imagine someone eating perhaps two and one-half pounds of bread a day, with very little in the way of meat or fish or dairy foods. You woud also have to imagine (and "imagine" is the especially appropriate word here) that one of the nutrients reduced in amount during milling and *not* restored in fortified bread is in fact likely to be so much reduced as to cause deficiency. This might be a nutrient such as pyridoxine or manganese, deficiencies of which are virtually unknown in human diets.

If sugar contributes significantly to the causation of the diseases of affluence, and importantly to the causation of coronary thrombosis, this is not because refined sugar has any different effects from those of brown sugar. But it does indirectly have something to do with sugar refining, because there is a wide range of products that are made with refined sugar.

If people insisted on taking only brown sugar and products made with brown sugar, most of them would, at the end of the day, have eaten very much less sugar. In the days before sugar was as highly refined as it is today, it was palatable in tea only if peach and other flavors were added as well.

I said in Chapter 3 that brown sugar has no health advantage over white sugar, but also that it is better for you to eat brown than white sugar. I think you can now understand this apparent contradiction. Brown sugar gives you no realistic amounts of nutrients, so it is not nutritionally superior to white sugar. On the other hand, you cannot possibly eat as much brown sugar as you can white sugar, so the harmful effects of sugar that I shall be describing cannot be so great if all your sugar is brown.

For quite different reasons, you can absolve the process of flour refining from any participation in the increase in the number of people suffering from coronary thrombosis or other diseases of affluence, at least since the beginning of the century. The bread Westerners eat today has been made from much the same sort of flour since the time of the introduction of roller milling in the 1870s. Its fiber content has not changed, nor has its content of protein; the only real change has been the introduction of fortification. In Britain, there has been since 1946 a compulsory addition of calcium, iron, and two vitamins of the B group: nicotinic acid (niacin) and thiamine (vitamin B_1).

In America, bread need not have nutrients added. If it does, it is called "enriched," and must contain riboflavin (vitamin B_2) as well as thiamine, niacin, and iron. And, just as now, most of the bread eaten since the end of the last century has been white bread.

Not only has there been no change in the sort of flour from which bread is made; there has been a considerable reduction in the amount of bread consumed. In America, total consumption of wheat flour has fallen from an annual average of 217 pounds in 1909 to 110 pounds in 1970. In 1900, Britons ate an average of fifteen ounces of bread per day; in 1953, it was twelve ounces; in 1971, it was five ounces.

In both countries, the amount is falling all the time. It is difficult, therefore, to see how the eating of white bread can be an important cause of diseases that have been increasing during the same time that people have been eating less and less of what has basically been the same white bread.

By all means eat brown bread, or brown sugar, if that is what you want to do. But don't kid yourself that brown is beautiful. There is no room for color prejudice in nutrition, not any more than there is anywhere else in our lives.

Quite early on, I said that there is cause for concern about diets today. But there is no point in worrying about imaginary dangers. If you do, you will be likely to go on overlooking the real dangers.

5

Who Eats Sugar, and How Much?

People look at me quite incredulously when I tell them that there are now many parts of the world where the average person—man, woman, and child— is eating more than one hundred pounds of sugar a year —two pounds or more a week. This amounts to more than one-sixth of the total diet. But though this is true today, it has only rather recently become so and it still isn't true for all countries. In this chapter, I want to show how sugar consumption has been changing; how much is being eaten in different countries and by people of different ages; and how much of Western man's consumption is ingested by way of different sorts of manufactured foods and drinks, along with the sugar to which people help themselves from the bowl at the table.

Before going any further, I should emphasize that in this book I am talking about the sugar (sucrose) produced from the cane and the beet. This is technically called centrifugal sugar. I am excluding sucrose produced from other sources such as the maple and the palm; the amounts are negligible and come to only 1 percent or so of the total. I am also excluding milk sugar (lactose) and the sucrose and other sugars one consumes in fruit and vegetables. The reason here is also chiefly quantitative; the amounts of centrifugal sugar are much greater than those of sucrose from other sources. In one of our studies, we found that adults ate about half of their total carbohydrate as starch, 35 percent as centrifugal sucrose, 7 percent as lactose, and the remaining 8 percent or so as the mixed sugars in fruits and vegetables—mostly glucose, fructose, and sucrose.

In the year 1850, world production of sugar was about one and one-half million tons. Forty years later, it was more than 5 million tons, and by the turn of the century it was more than 11 million tons. Except for a setback during each of the two world wars, production has continued to rise rapidly, so that it reached 35 million tons by 1950 and is now over 70 million tons. Over the past 150 years, there has been a fifty-fold increase in world sugar production; allowing for the increase in world population, this represents an increase in average consumption from three pounds a year to forty-five pounds. The most extensive statistics of sugar production and consumption were collected ten years ago in a report produced for the Food and Agriculture Organization of the United Nations. Although this is now a little out of date, I shall quote some of its findings because they still demonstrate many interesting features that are not easy to discover from more recent statistics.

During the twenty years from 1938 to 1958, there was an increase in world production of many commodities. Among food items, cocoa increased by 20 percent, milk by about 30 percent, meat and food grains up to 50 percent; but sugar production outstripped all of these with its enormous increase: 100 percent during the twenty years. Between 1900 and 1957, consumption of sugar increased from an average of eleven pounds a year to thirty-four pounds; by now, as I said, it is about forty-five pounds. But the increase has differed in different countries. It has been most rapid in the countries that until recently had a low consumption.

Before the last war, Italy's yearly average was less than twenty pounds; by 1970 it was more than sixty pounds. Those countries that already had a high consumption have had a smaller increase or none at all; in the United Kingdom there was an increase from about 100 pounds to 120 pounds, while in the United States there has been no change from the previous 102.5 pounds or so. It looks as if there is a limit of somewhat over 100 pounds a head a year at which all countries stop increasing their intake. The wealthier countries gradually achieved this high level by a slow and fairly steady increase over perhaps 200 years; the poorer countries are now achieving it very much more rapidly.

Just over 200 years ago, the United Kingdom's consumption of sugar was only four or five pounds a year. By the middle of the nineteenth century, this figure had increased to about twenty-five pounds a year in the U.K., and sugar consumption for the United States (for which earlier figures are not available) was forty pounds a year. With the 1970 sugar intake in the U.K. at 120 pounds and in the U.S. at 102 pounds, the last 100 years has seen an almost five-fold increase in sugar consumption in Britain and an increase of almost two-and-a-half times in the U.S.

Here are some figures for other countries or populations. In Switzerland, average intake has increased tenfold in the last 100 years. Consumption among Canadian Eskimos increased much more rapidly; in one area, it rose from twenty-six pounds to 104 pounds a year between 1959 and 1967. The consumption among the rural Zulu population in South Africa increased ten-fold in eleven years, from six pounds a year to sixty pounds a year between 1953 and 1964.

I have been discussing the way sugar consumption has been going up, especially during the last 200 years or so, and also the way sugar consumption differs in different countries—generally high in wealthy countries and low in poor countries. I should like to say a little more about diets in rich countries and in poor countries because, although not directly related to sugar consumption, they do have a bearing on sugar intake; they also give a better picture of the way diets are affected by income. Let us look at the diets in different countries according to the average national income, and calculate how many calories were supplied by these diets; how much protein, fat, and carbohydrate; and how much the carbohydrate was made up of sugar on the one hand and of other components—chiefly starch—on the other hand.

As one moves from the poorest to the wealthiest groups of countries, one finds an increase from about 2,000 calories a day to about 3,000. Protein increases by about 80 percent, from fifty grams a day to ninety grams, and fat increases about four-fold, from thirty-five grams to 140 grams. The total amount of carbohydrate is much the same, irrespective of wealth, except in the very poorest countries, where you can say they just have too little of everything.

More interesting than this similarity in total carbohydrate consumption is the very considerable change in the kinds of carbohydrate you encounter as you pass from poor to rich countries. There is a great increase in the amount of sugar, and a corresponding fall in the remaining carbohydrate, mostly starch. This is similar to the situation when a particular country becomes increasingly wealthy: more sugar is eaten—and less bread, or rice, or corn, or other starchy food.

The figures I have given so far are averages for whole populations. When I tell an audience in London that they eat five ounces of sugar a day, they profess astonished disbelief. Everyone insists that he eats much less than this, so I usually say that since five ounces is the daily average there must be other people who are eating more. Unfortunately, almost no precise figures exist for variations between individuals. In our own studies, we measured how much sugar is being taken by various groups of older children and by men and women of different ages. They are not necessarily representative, but I give you our results because they demonstrate some general features.

Let me add that it is likely that we are underestimating the exact consumption, because people tend to forget the occasional sugar drink or piece of chocolate they have been taking. Still, one can get some interesting information even if it is approximate.

Comparing men and women of different ages, the most striking feature is the very high consumption of teenage boys: more than 50 percent above that of teenage girls. The sex difference persists throughout later life, although not so strikingly. From the age of twenty, men take something like 15 percent or 20 percent more sugar than do women. This is possibly because women are more weight-conscious, so they deliberately restrict their sugar consumption. A decline of sugar intake sets in with increasing age, so that people in their sixties take about one-third less sugar than do people in their twenties.

These figures come from our own studies, but I have also tried to find statistics reported by others.

Mostly, however, they are statistics for only some sugar items.

The U.S. Agricultural Research Service in March 1969 reported that the highest consumption of sugar and sweets (excluding syrup, honey, and molasses) is by children of twelve to fourteen: forty-nine grams a day for boys and forty-three grams for girls. At twenty to thirty-four years, the daily intake is thirty-seven grams for men, thirty-one for women. Over sixty-five years of age, the figure has gone down to twenty-nine grams for women but has gone up to forty grams for men.

In Scotland, dentists examined thirteen-year-old boys and girls, a younger age group than any we have studied. They estimated only the amount of candy the children ate, and they added that they were sure that their figures were in fact under-estimates. The average weekly intake was seventeen and one-half ounces, boys eating slightly more than girls. Eight percent of the children, however, took more than thirty-two ounces a week.

These figures are equivalent to a daily intake of about 2 ounces (55 grams) a day of sugar for all the children, and nearly 4 ounces (105 grams) for 8 percent of the children. The average intake of candy for the whole British population is eight ounces a week, which is, incidentally, higher than that for any other country. It seems likely that the thirteen-year-olds ate not only twice as much candy as the national average, but also substantially more in the way of cakes and puddings and sugar with their breakfast cereals.

Even by a conservative estimate, these can be expected to bring the total amount of sugar to something like 50 percent more than the national average. This would make the total consumption of a thirteen-year-old about seven and one-half ounces of sugar a day, which would supply 850 calories out of their daily total intake of about 3,000 calories. Now think of the children who eat not seventeen and one-half ounces of sweets a week but more than thirty-two ounces, and it is pretty certain that there must be a lot of children getting at least half of their calories from sugar.

You might perhaps think that by eating a lot of sugar between meals they would cut down the sugar in meals. Not at all. A colleague of mine recently found that the midday meals in several English schools contained sugar giving about 25 percent of the calories, and on the whole children get the same sorts of food in schools that they might be getting at home. So it does look as if children get more than the average amount of sugar, sometimes much more, not only in the snacks and drinks between meals, but also in the meals themselves. Part of this, I am sure, is due to the attitudes of their mothers: to give pleasure to their children; to win their affection; to provide them—as they erroneously believe—with the energy they need for growth and work and play.

There was recently reported in the London *Times* the case of a young lad eating more than six and one-half pounds of sugar a week, which amounts to nearly 350 pounds a year. The report was by his dentist, who complained that six months after his mouth had been made quite free from decay, it was now once more full of rotting teeth. Our own record comes from a fifteen-year-old boy who also consumed just under one pound of sugar a day, or around 1,700 calories.

Of course, just as there are some people who eat very much more than the average amount of sugar, there must be those who eat less than the average. Our own figures suggest that the range of variation of sugar intake is far greater than the range for most other foods. We have found people taking as little as half an ounce a day (15 grams) as well as those taking as much as fourteen ounces a day (400 grams); the latter are eating in one day what the former eat in a month.

Altogether, I find it difficult to resist the conclusion that, whereas the national average consumption of sugar in the U.S. and the U.K. represents something like 17 percent or 18 percent of the average calorie intake, the average for children would work out at around 25 percent of the calories or even a little more. And again let me say that there must be some who are getting 50 percent of their calories from sugar. In absolute terms sugar consumption for many children must amount to nearer ten ounces a day than the five-ounce national average.

In case you think that I am exaggerating the amount of sugar taken by children, let me quote from an advertisement by Sugar Information, the public relations organization for the American sugar industry. Forget for now the reference to obesity. I shall be saying something more about this aspect of sugar later. Here is part of the advertisement:

You've probably had people tell you they're avoiding this or that because it has sugar in it. If you want to see how much sense there is to that idea, next time you pass a bunch of kids, take a look. Kids eat and drink more things made with sugar than anybody. But how many fat ones do you see?

Good nutrition comes from a balanced diet. One that provides the right amounts, and right kinds, of protein, vitamins, minerals, fats and carbohydrates. Sugar is an important carbohydrate. In moderation, sugar has a place in a balanced diet.

The word I like best in this advertisement is "moderation." But would you really accept as moderate the current average consumption of sugar by kids, probably amounting to 25 percent or more of their calories and adding up to seven ounces or so a day?

Let me pursue this concept of moderation, which is heard so often. Supposing we were living a couple of hundred years ago. People in America and Britain were then eating an average of a couple of ounces of sugar a week. If someone were then to have said that you should eat sugar in moderation, you would have thought in terms of perhaps no more than three ounces a week. You would certainly have protested that seven ounces a week—one ounce a day—was a quite excessive amount. But people today accept *five* ounces a day as moderate, so only when someone eats even much more than this does it become generally accepted that he is eating immoderately.

Look now at babies, who are more and more bottle-fed, even though there is a slight drift back to breast feeding in some middle-class homes. The commonest formula consists of dried cow's milk, perhaps modified in some way, to which is added sugar. Except in a few sensible preparations, the sugar that is added is sucrose, not lactose (milk sugar), and I shall show later that this is not at all the same in its effect on the baby. Here I refer only to the disadvantage of sugar's having a much sweeter taste than lactose, so that a baby is inducted into his later sugar-rich life by being encouraged to develop a taste for maximum sweetness.

As soon as a baby begins to receive mixed feeding—and this is often at two or three months or even earlier—he will begin to have cereals, and then foods like egg yolk and chopped meat and strained vegetables and fruit. Mother will almost certainly add sugar to the cereal and to the fruit (although it is by no means uncommon at least for a British mother to add it also to egg and meat and fish). And I have not mentioned the pernicious habit of giving babies pacifiers that have a reservoir for syrup or pacifiers that are from time to time dipped into the sugar bowl.

I know of a family of four people: father, mother, a girl of four, and a baby of six months. They buy and use eleven pounds of sugar a week, and this does not prevent them from also buying the usual assortment of cookies and ice creams and other manufactured foods and drinks with sugar. The baby certainly gets less than a quarter of all this, but it is hardly deprived, since it is one of those that has its pacifier dipped into the family sugar bowl.

One of the reasons why some people find it difficult to accept that on average Americans and Britons eat two pounds of sugar or more a week is that they think only of the sugar that is brought into the home as visible sugar. But an increasing proportion of sugar is now bought already made up into foods by the manufacturer. If you look at your own sugar consumption, you will see that over the years chances are that a smaller and smaller fraction is household sugar and a greater and greater fraction is industrial sugar. (Household sugar is mostly what is bought by the housewife, but also includes the much smaller quantity bought for use in cafés and restaurants. Industrial sugar goes to the factory and comes to us in the form of candy, ice cream, soft drinks, cakes, cookies, and nowadays also in a very wide range of other items, especially the fancily packaged "convenience foods.")

The poorer countries, as you might expect, consume less of their sugar in the industrial form; manufactured foods are a luxury consumed increasingly in the

wealthier countries. In the late 50s, according to the
FAO report I mentioned earlier, South Africa took
only 20 percent of its sugar in manufactured foods,
France took 40 percent, and Australia 55 percent.
American manufactured sugar increased from less than
30 percent in 1927 to about 50 percent in 1957, and
I see is now more than 70 percent. The increase in
the proportion of manufactured sugar in the U.S. is
especially interesting in view of the fact that the total
sugar consumption had not changed much over this
period.

The ways in which sugar is used by food manufacturers in the U.S. and the U.K., and the proportion
of those uses, is shown in the table. But I want to
amplify these figures in several ways. To begin with, I
believe there are several reasons why Westerners continue to increase their consumption of manufactured
foods containing sugar. One is that any efficient manufacturer is constantly producing more and more attractive foods. Because of competition, he keeps making
new products or new variations on his old products,
each time with a purpose of producing something that
is even more attractive than before. More and more,
people find it difficult to resist these delicious foods and
drinks. In 1969, more than 150 different kinds of candy
were advertised on television in England at a cost of
more than $25 million.

Secondly, sugar offers many more properties than
sweetness alone. Its use in different sorts of candy
depends also on its bulk, on its ability to exist either
in crystallized or noncrystallized form, on its solubility
in water, and on its change of color and flavor when it
is heated. Its use in jams depends on its ability to set
in the presence of pectin, and on its high osmotic pressure so that growth of molds and bacteria is inhibited.

In small quantities, sugar seems to enhance the flavor of other foods without necessarily adding specifically to sweetness. These and many other properties of sugar amount to an extraordinary versatility and account for its use in such a vast range of foods and drinks.

The result is plain to see if you walk around the supermarket as I did, and make a list of foods with sugar among their ingredients. Leaving aside obvious foods like cakes, cookies, desserts, and soft drinks, you will find sugar in almost every variety of canned soups, in many cans of baked beans and pastas, many kinds of canned meat, almost every breakfast food, several frozen vegetables and made-up dishes, and most canned vegetables. In some of these foods, especially in the foods like meats or vegetarian meat substitutes, the amounts of sugar are quite small. But in many foods, the amount is really surprisingly high. You can get some idea by seeing where sugar ranks in the list of ingredients. If it is first in the list, the food contains more sugar than any other ingredient. This was true of one or two canned soups, and one or two breakfast foods. It was also true of several pickles and sauces.

A third reason why people increasingly buy manufactured foods containing sugar is that they increasingly buy foods in "convenience" form—usually items that they would previously have made for themselves. And it looks from my sampling as if these foods are likely to contain more sugar than the housewife would have used. The manufacturer seems to have found, or at any rate convinced himself, that people like sugar with everything, and more and more of it. In the last two or three years, I have found it difficult at a bar to get tomato juice, my favorite "tipple," that has not had sugar added to it. I am also rather fond of peanut butter, but the manufacturers of the two most popular brands in

England have now decided that I ought to have it with sugar.

Here let me give one good mark to the health-food people; at least some do not put sugar into their peanut butter—anyway, not yet.

If you want to test what I am saying, try next time you are out for the day to get a drink of something or other that is not alcoholic, does not contain sugar, and is not a specially advertised "diet drink."

It does seem to be true that until they reach a certain limit most people demand more and more sugar as they go on taking it. Certainly the converse is true. Many people have been restricting sugar for some time, either because they are concerned about their weight, or for even more serious reasons; now when for social reasons these people do have to take sugary foods and drinks, they often find them intolerably sweet. At his third birthday, my well-brought-up grandson Benjamin took one bite of his iced birthday cake and ate no more because, he said, "It's too sweet."

What is to me surprising is the high proportion of sugar in many so-called health foods (apart from the peanut butter I mentioned). As I have said, and as I shall explain in more detail later, there is no special virtue in brown or raw sugars, so I simply draw attention to the fact that sugar appears to figure prominently in foods that are supposed to be "good for you." Eggs and bacon, or the old-fashioned British favorite, kipper, would be better for you than several of the special breakfast health foods.

One more reason why Westerners eat so much sugar is that increasing affluence gives people more leisure during which they are sitting in front of the television or making a trip in their car: conditions that lend themselves to the consumption of snacks and soft drinks, which again are nowadays so easily available and considered to be inexpensive. And snacks usually, and soft drinks almost always, are rich sources of sugar.

Another point about soft drinks. When I was young, and I was thirsty, I had a glass of water. Nowadays when a child is thirsty, it seems almost obligatory that he quench his thirst with some sugar-laden cola or other drink. And this is often true for adults too, although it is just as likely to be an alcoholic drink like beer. In this way, sugar is consumed almost inadvertently. The modern trend for drinks like tonic water or bitter lemon as mixers is for many people still a further source of sugar of which they are hardly aware. Two small bottles with your gin or vodka, and you have swallowed an ounce or more of sugar.

Life is increasingly difficult for people who, like myself, want to avoid sugar, and particularly for those who, like the people with hereditary fructose intolerance, get sick when they take sugar.

What I find especially worrying is the use of so much sugar in foods made for babies. And again I am talking not only of desserts, or even breakfast cereal mixes. There is sugar in a large proportion of the meat and vegetable preparations in baby foods and junior foods. If, as seems likely, people are laying the foundations for serious disease in later life by encouraging the development of a sweet tooth in children, this may be doing them even more harm than if they were encouraged to begin smoking at the age of twelve or fifteen.

6

Sugar's Calories Make You Thin—They Say

The inclusion of large amounts of sugar can affect one's diet in two ways. It can be taken *in addition* to the normal diet; or *instead* of a caloric equivalent in food. More likely than either of these alone, it can be done both ways: by adding something to the total calories and also displacing some other foods. Since, as I showed, sugar supplies nearly one-fifth of the average eater's calories, no aspect of sugar consumption can be ignored. Its effects will be particularly evident in those many people whose intake of sugar is appreciably greater than the average.

The consumption of sugar on top of an ordinary diet increases the risk of obesity; the consumption of sugar instead of part of an adequate diet increases the risk of nutritional deficiencies. In this chapter, I want to deal with the question of sugar consumption leading to an increase in caloric intake.

I have already pointed out that the average intake of sugar in America or Britain supplies some 500 to 550 calories a day. But this is not the whole picture. Many people take at least twice as much as the average of four and one-half or five ounces a day; they would be getting at least 1,000 calories a day from sugar, and 1,500 calories or even more is not unknown. This sounds enormous, but I am not counting visible sugar alone. These people consume only part of this daily quota as sugar by itself. Much would be taken with other foods that supply lots of calories: cocoa in chocolate, fat in ice cream, fat and flour in cookies and cakes. They would then be getting even more calories than the figures I have just given.

This book is not about obesity and its causes and treatment. So I shall mention only two matters that are particularly relevant to the question of sugar—one obvious, one less obvious and even, in part, controversial. The obvious one is that people take sweet foods and drinks because they like them. And just as you will eat less than you need if your food is unpalatable and unappetizing, so you will eat more than you need if it is especially appetizing.

Let me remind you of some of the points I made in Chapter 2. Most often, people eat chocolate or cake because they are tempted by their appearance and taste, and not so much because they really need those extra calories. And when people take sugary soft drinks, they usually do so because they are thirsty rather than because they are hungry, even though the drinks supply lots of calories (that are probably not needed) along with the water that *is* needed.

The second point I want to make is in answer to those who consume quite a lot of sugar but are not overweight. I think there are three reasons why this can happen. The first would apply to those whose sugar intake is matched by a corresponding reduction in other foods, so that they are not taking excessive calories (though, as I shall show, they may be running the risk of nutritional deficiency). The second reason is that they may be extremely active people, so that they take a lot of calories but also use them up.

The third reason why people may eat a lot of sugar and still not put on weight is the controversial reason I mentioned. There is now evidence that some lucky people's bodies have the facility of burning off surplus calories; their metabolism is increased by just the equivalent of the extra calories they take, and so they do not put on weight. I know that this view is not universally accepted in the textbooks of physiology and nutrition, but I must say I find the evidence quite convincing. Even these people, of course, have a limit to the number of surplus calories they can dispose of in this way, so they, too, will put on weight if their intake of calories is in excess of disposal.

If you are one of the lucky ones who can get rid of excessive calories from sugar, you may not get fat, but by no means will you escape its other ill effects. Tooth decay, indigestion, diabetes, coronary thrombosis, and all the other conditions I shall discuss—these are not necessarily avoided by people who can eat lots of sugar without getting fat.

So there is no point in worrying whether or not everyone agrees about the thesis that metabolism can increase in response to an increase of food consumption. Suffice it to say that you cannot help getting fat if you are taking in more calories than you can dispose of. You simply have to add that a very obvious and potent cause of excessive calories is the consumption of foods and drinks that contain sugar, largely because people find them so delicious.

It may be that you are one of those who finds it

difficult to accept that sugar can be important in producing overweight. In America especially, an intensive advertising and public relations campaign has been in progress for several years to convince the public that sugar has nothing to do with obesity. First you are told that a spoon of sugar contains only eighteen calories.

The sugar industry's advertisments say:

"Sugar's got what it takes. Only 18 calories to the teaspoon. And it's all ENERGY."

This is quite true, provided you use a rather small spoon and make sure it is a level spoonful rather than the more usual heaped spoonful. Our research experience shows that most people take the sort of spoonful that gives them more like thirty calories than eighteen calories.

You might want to work out how much sugar you take just in tea and coffee. Suppose you take an average number of cups, which is about six a day. Suppose you take the not ridiculously high amount of two spoons a cup, each giving "only" twenty-five calories. That is 50 calories a cup, and 300 calories at the end of the day. This is what the whole truth is likely to be, rather than the partial and misleading truth about eighteen calories a spoon.

There is another point. Not only do the sugar people tell you that sugar does not make you fat; they say it actually helps to make you slim. Their argument goes like this:

The reason people get hungry is that they have a low level of glucose in the blood. If you eat sugar, you stop being hungry because it is very rapidly digested and absorbed, so that the level of glucose in the blood rises. Have a little sugar from time to time, then, and you will end up by eating less, and so reduce your weight.

Here is another quote from one of the sugar people's advertisements:

> Willpower fans, the search is over!
> And guess where it's at? In sugar!
> Sugar works faster than any other food to turn your appetite down, turn energy up.
> Spoil your appetite with sugar, and you could come up with willpower.
> Sugar—only 18 calories per teaspoon, and it's all energy.

Unfortunately, there are three flaws in this argument.

The first is the idea that your eating is controlled by the level of your blood sugar. This is still only a theory. There is quite a lot of evidence in favor of this theory, but there is also a lot of evidence that it may not be correct, or at least that it is not a complete explanation of what controls hunger.

Secondly, even if the theory is correct, science has no idea how much sugar you might need in order to make inroads on your appetite. And in any case there is no reason to believe that sugar will affect your appetite any more than any other food will, just because it is absorbed quickly.

Thirdly, there is absolutely no evidence at all that the sugar reduces your hunger to an extent greater than the calories you get from the sugar.

Suppose you have just taken two spoons of sugar in each of two cups of coffee, and thus gained 100 calories. You are now less hungry, so you eat less. But by how much? One-hundred calories? Fifty calories? Three-hundred calories? The only evidence I know suggests that your appetite is reduced by *less* than the number of calories you have taken from the sugar. This evidence came from some tests I carried out a few years ago. I did these tests because the same lose-weight-by-eating-more story was being noised about, though not for ordinary sugar (sucrose), but for glucose. The idea was that you took about one-third of an ounce of glucose three times a day a little while before each meal. Then you followed a calorie-restricted diet, and you were supposed to be able to do this more easily because the glucose had reduced your hunger.

What I did was to take two groups of overweight people and put them on the same calorie-reduced diet —the diet in fact given by the manufacturers of the glucose tablets. At the end of six weeks, people taking the glucose did indeed lose weight, a matter of six and three-quarter pounds. But the people on the same diet without the glucose lost about eleven and one-half pounds—nearly five pounds more, or close to twice as much.

You might think, then, that the glucose did nothing at all; you might suppose that the people who consumed it ate the same amount of their diet as the others did, but the extra calories from the glucose made them lose less. But in fact this would only account for about one pound of the difference, not the five pounds or so that we found. The only explanation that remains is that the glucose tablets actually *increased* the amount that people ate on their calorie-restricted diet—exactly the opposite of what it was supposed to do.

I suppose it is natural for the vast and powerful sugar interests to seek to protect themselves, since in the wealthier countries sugar makes a greater contribution to our diets, measured in calories, than does meat or bread or any other single commodity. But what is always sad is to see scientists being persuaded to support the sort of claims I have just described.

Is it because they like sugar just as much as other

people do? Or is it because at least some of them have still not gotten around to accepting the idea that all the carbohydrates don't behave in the same way in the body? Or is it that they have persuaded themselves (and then broadcast to the public) that the modern scourge is too much fat in the diet, and so they now have difficulty in admitting that they may have been wrong?

It is equally difficult to see why nutritionists should endorse the consumption of sugar at the present levels. What with the high incidence of obesity, there is no acceptable reason for recommending that sugar intake should *not* be reduced, or that it should be reduced only as part of a general reduction of food. It is, after all, the only food that supplies nothing whatever in the way of nutrients; it is, remember, the claim of the sugar refiners themselves that their product is virtually 100 percent pure. It supplies nothing whatever other than calories, and calories are all that matter in weight reduction.

Cutting down any other food—*any* other food—is bound to reduce nutrients as well as calories. There is no evidence that overweight people are taking an excess of nutrients; but there is quite a lot of evidence to suggest that some of them could do with a nutritionally better-balanced diet. I shall have more to say about this question of calories and nutrients in the next chapter.

The proof of the pudding is in the eating—or, in this case, in the not eating. Many people lose excessive weight very successfully simply by giving up sugar, or by severely restricting it. If you take only one spoon of sugar in each cup of coffee, and you drink only five cups a day, you could lose more than ten pounds of weight in a year just by eliminating the sugar in your coffee.

Sometimes, in order to reduce their weight to acceptable levels, people also need to restrict starchy foods, and so adopt a strict low-carbohydrate diet. Of course, giving up sugar and starchy foods and drinks requires some self-discipline, as does any alteration in dietary habits. But for several reasons, which I have described in detail in my earlier book, *The Slimming Business,* the low-carbohydrate diet is the most sensible and effective way of controlling body weight. And my colleagues and I have demonstrated by experiment, not simply by armchair calculation, that the supply of nutrients through this method is far better than in the orthodox method that tells you to eat the same as before, only less.

I have never really understood why so many doctors in the American medical and nutritional establishment have frowned upon a diet that tells you in effect to reduce only, or chiefly, those foods that give you the calories you *don't* need while giving you so little of the nutrients you *do* need.

Although I said I was not going to go into details about the principles of obesity, I must add one important point about babies. I have already mentioned the increasingly common custom of adding sugar not only to milk formulas but also to the cereal and other foods on which babies are weaned. The result, as you can see everywhere, is the increasing number of fat babies, so much so that pediatric authorities in the United States and even the Chief School Medical Officer in England have frequently drawn attention to this problem.

It seems that over-feeding in very young babies does not simply put more fat into their existing fat cells; it also makes their little bodies *produce* a greater number of fat cells. One of the factors that appears to control your appetite is the amount of fat in each of your cells; when the cells lose some of their fat, you feel hungry.

Obviously, if you have lots of cells, you will still have a larger *total* amount of fat, even when *each* of them has an amount low enough to make you feel hungry. Then, as an adult, you will be one of those miserable fat people who can diet only with great difficulty, and by going hungry, and get their weight right down to what it should be—only to regain it with demoralizing speed. Fat babies not only grow into fat adults; they grow into fat adults with real diet problems.

7

How To Eat More Calories
Without Eating Real Food

A criticism that one hears frequently of refined sugar is that it supplies "empty calories." This is true. The critics often go on to say that the refining process is at fault in that it removes essential nutrients that are present in unrefined sugar in significant amounts. This is not true, as I showed in Chapter 4.

Having considered what happens when you take sugar in *addition* to your other foods, I'd like now to look at what happens when you take it *instead* of some of your other foods. After all, if people take 500 calories a day as sugar, and sometimes much more, it is likely that there will be some reduction in other foods; there must be a limit to how much even the most gluttonous person can eat.

In the simplest situation, imagine a diet of 2,500 calories a day made up largely of good nutritious foods like meat and cheese and milk and fish and fruit and vegetables, with some potatoes and bread and breakfast cereal—and only a little of these last foods if you are on a low-carbohydrate diet. Now keep the calories at 2,500 but replace 500 or 550 of them with sugar, the average amount taken in a day. I have shown that you can usually do this simply by adding only moderate amounts of sugar to your tea and coffee, and taking an occasional sugar-sweetened soft drink. Clearly, the result of this replacement of 20 percent of your calories by sugar would be a reduction in your intake of nutrients—protein, all vitamins, all mineral elements—also by 20 percent.

No nutritional deficiency will occur if your previous diet contained an excess of 20 percent of all the nutrients you require. But suppose it did not contain this surplus. More important, suppose that you were one of those who takes more than the average amount of sugar—equal perhaps to 30 percent of your calories, or even 40 percent. Now it begins to be more difficult, as you can see, to imagine that the diet of 2,500 calories, which originally supplied as much of the nutrients as you need, will still do so when the foods supplying them are reduced by 30 percent or 40 percent.

This does not mean that by eating four and one-half or five ounces of sugar a day—or even seven or eight ounces—you would be rapidly heading for pellagra, beri-beri, or scurvy. In extreme cases, with quite a lot of sugar and with the remainder of the diet not too well constructed, such diseases do occasionally occur. (I shall later refer to the role of sugar in producing full-fledged protein deficiency in poor countries.) But it may very well occur that your diet is marginally insufficient in nutritional terms, so that you are in that twilight zone between excellent health and a manifest deficiency disease such as those I have mentioned. Not quite well; tired and easily exhausted; prone to aches and pains and odd infections. All these vague but very real symptoms occur in all of us at some time or another. But while being a bit under par is no proof that your diet is deficient, nutritional deficiency must be considered as a possible cause in people whose diets are unbalanced by a large intake of sugar.

Is there any way of showing that sugar can really— not just hypothetically—push more desirable foods out of one's diet? One way of finding this out, I thought, was to check the trends of consumption of different sorts of food, especially those that are universally recognized as highly nutritious. About six years ago, I decided to look at the trends of meat and fruit especially, and for two reasons. First, they fall into the category of highly nutritious foods, and secondly, for most people they are also highly palatable. I argued that the increase in the consumption of sugar-containing foods, because they, too, are very palatable, might show itself by a reduction in the consumption of meat and fruit.

I must break off to explain why, when you look at the relevant statistics, you have to bear in mind two important considerations. The first is that, although *total* sugar consumption in America levelled off some thirty or forty years ago, and in Britain in the last three or four years, there was a simultaneous decline in the use of sugar in the home and an increase in the amount of sugar used in manufactured foods. Crudely, and not completely accurately, one can say that people are putting less sugar in beverages at home but take more sugar in ice cream and cakes and cookies, where, incidentally, it comes with plenty of other calories. You would then expect the effects of sugar in pushing other foods out of the diet to be increasing, even though the absolute amount of the sugar itself is stationary.

The second point to bear in mind is that meat and

fruit, besides being among the nutritionist's favorites, are also relatively expensive, so that, especially in the bad old days, there was more consumed by wealthy people than by poorer people. This social gradient has declined in the Western world with increasing affluence; the poorer sections of the population are not as poor as they used to be. So what nutritionists and economists have been predicting is that general increasing affluence would bring about an increasing consumption of meat and fruit. One would expect little or no change in consumption by the wealthier groups of the population, who presumably were always able to eat as much of these desirable foods as they wished; on the other hand, one would expect a great rise in the amounts that poorer groups consume as their economic situation improves.

So what about my hunch that sugar and sugar-rich foods are driving these better foods out of our diets?

The difficulty was to get the right statistics. We needed not just trends in average consumption for a whole population but the consumption of similar fractions of the populations—both a wealthy and a poorer fraction—at two different times. Eventually we had to be content with figures for fruit consumption in America, and meat consumption in Britain.

My colleagues and I were able to compare the amount of fruit eaten in 1942 with that eaten in 1956 by the wealthiest 20 percent of Americans and the poorest 30 percent. As we had expected, the poorest group was eating more fruit—3 pounds a week instead of 2½—but the wealthiest group was eating significantly less—4.7 pounds instead of 5.6. In the U.K., we had a more difficult job because the basis of collecting the statistics had changed. But when we made the appropriate adjustment, we were able to compare meat consumption in 1936 and in 1960 of the poorer half of the population and the wealthiest tenth. We found that the poorer half was taking about 8 percent more meat than formerly while the wealthiest one-tenth was taking 14 percent less.

Indeed, we need hardly have done this elaborate calculation for meat in the U.K. Everyone with any experience of the country before World War II knows that the poorer people ate little meat; there were, for example, the famous studies of John Boyd Orr. Yet in spite of a sizable increase among the poorer people, average meat consumption in the U.K. has hardly changed since before the war. This can only have been due to a *decrease* in consumption by the wealthier people.

More recent evidence comes from the U.S., where, as you probably know, there has been a considerable outcry by experts in the last few years about the existence of nutritional deficiencies. How much of a deficiency exists is uncertain. What *is* certain is that it is much more than most people had thought. The most revealing statistics are those that show that between 1955 and 1965 there was a 10 percent increase in the number of family diets whose content of nutrients fell below the levels recommended by the Food and Nutrition Board of the National Research Council.

While it is true that the cost of food had gone up by 16 percent during that period, average incomes had gone up by 23 percent, so that it is unlikely that the fall in the nutritional quality of the average American diet was due to increased economic hardship. The more likely explanation, I believe, is again that some of the nutritionally good foods were crowded out by the nutritionally inferior, sugar-based foods. This is also the belief of Dr. Joan Courtless, a member of the U.S. Department of Agriculture, who says:

> The surveys themselves show that it [*the worsening of diets*] lies in the choice being made—increased consumption of soft drinks and decreased consumption of milk; increased consumption of snacks and decreased consumption of vegetables and fruit.

And you will remember that snacks contain very large amounts of sugar.

What does all this have to do with refined sugar and unrefined sugar?

Many people believe that the danger of nutritional deficiencies comes from eating sugar that has been refined; they say that if only we ate unrefined sugar, we should be getting all the nutrients we require, and in adequate quantities. I have already shown that the amounts of nutrients supplied by brown sugar, or even by raw sugar, are ridiculously inadequate to make any real contribution to the diet. But people still have this rather mystical belief that unrefined sugar is "whole" and "natural," so that it "must be" nutritious and complete. However, if you look back to what I said about how sugar is produced, you will see that the only thing that is whole or complete is the sugar cane or the sugar beet. You obviously can't eat the sugar cane, though you can chew it. And I promise you that you simply cannot eat sugar beet or chew it; it is horrible. Nor can you eat raw beet sugar.

You could, I suppose, eat raw cane sugar, although it is pretty filthy. But I showed that raw cane sugar is very much a manufactured product, and it requires relatively little more processing (another bad word, it seems) to turn raw sugar into refined sugar. To say that refined sugar is "processed" and "unnatural" and that raw

sugar is "unprocessed" and "natural" is about as sensible as to say that I am dressed if I am wearing all my
clothes including my tie, but that I become eligible to
join a nudist colony as soon as I take off my tie.

8

Can You Prove the Case?

If reading this book convinces you that sugar is in fact sweet and dangerous, you will certainly get involved in a lot of arguments when you come to convince other people. It will help you and stop your being thrown off balance if you carefully consider not only the facts I shall be giving you, but the wider problem of how to weigh evidence about the causes of disease, and how to form your final judgments about what really causes them. Before I begin to talk about diabetes and heart disease and duodenal ulcers and several other conditions, I should discuss this problem in general terms.

As you will see, quite a lot of the conclusions I shall be drawing in this book will inevitably be based partly on factual evidence and partly on personal judgment. Those of you who have attempted to follow reports on the enormous amount of research that has been done and is continuing into the problem of heart disease will not be surprised when I say that you have to mix objective facts and subjective opinion. Absolute proof of the cause or causes of any disease is very rare.

To get *absolute* proof that cigarette smoking causes

lung cancer, you would need to take, say, 1,000 young people at the age of fifteen; pair them off as carefully as you can into two very similar groups of 500 each; make one group smoke from that time onward; and rigidly prevent the other group from smoking. Then, after perhaps thirty or forty years, you can begin to see whether a significantly larger number of people in the smoking group have developed lung cancer.

Since this sort of experiment is clearly out of the question on ethical as well as practical grounds, it is necessary to examine evidence that is largely circumstantial, and to judge this against a background comprising, one hopes, rational and plausible general biological principles. I have tried to do this here. I have tried to recognize the limitations of all the evidence that is available, and in interpreting it I have tried to stand back and assess it chiefly on the basis of whether it makes sense, whether it fits in with what can be discerned about the rules that govern living processes and living organisms.

It is logical, then, to spend a few minutes looking at both of these aspects: to ascertain the kinds of evidence one can hope to find about the causes of disease, and the limitations of this evidence; and also to see if general laws can be detected that make sense in relation to the maintenance of health. Since I am talking in this book mostly about sugar, and since the most important disease I shall be talking about is heart disease, I shall refer briefly to sugar and heart disease, but the same principles apply to any cause and any disease.

I ought also to say just a little about the word "cause," because I am going to talk quite a lot about sugar being a "cause" of a number of diseases. In the first place, it is quite certain that none of the diseases I shall be talking about are *caused* by sugar in the same way that heat *causes* ice to melt. People differ in their susceptibility to disease, so that even in identical conditions—supposing you could produce them—one man might have a heart attack and another might not. This susceptibility seems to a large extent to be inherited, so one may say that your chances of getting a coronary are less if your parents, grandparents, uncles, and aunts have mostly lived to a ripe old age without having the disease; the chances are greater if many members of your family have had it.

In addition to this genetic factor, environmental factors also play a role in coronary disease. Most people accept the proposition that several environmental factors are influential, and that these include leading a sedentary sort of life and smoking cigarettes. What I am hoping to show is that eating a lot of sugar is another environmental factor (or cause) in producing heart disease. I do *not* propose to show that sugar is the one and only factor involved in producing this disease, or indeed, any disease.

One more word about cause. If an event *A* sets off another event *B*, and if without *A*, *B* would not occur, then you can call *A* the cause of *B*. But suppose I throw a lighted match into my waste-paper basket and my study and then my house burns down. Was the cause the lighted match? Or the loose paper in my waste-paper basket? Or the fact that my house contained lots of books and an excessive amount of wood?

If *any* one of these factors had been different, the house might not have burned down at all. Alternatively, there might have been a short circuit in the electrical supply to my desk lamp, so the house might burn for a reason quite different from that of a lighted match.

I could say that if I eat sugary foods, I get holes in

my teeth. Then presumably the sugary foods are the cause of dental decay. But I might not get dental decay, in spite of these foods, if I have a high genetic resistance to the disease; or if I brush my teeth immediately after eating these foods; or if I know how to keep my mouth free of the bacteria that actually attack the teeth after being stimulated to multiply and to become active by the sugar in food. Is sugar then "the" cause of tooth decay? Or is it the bacteria? Or the lack of resistance of my teeth?

So in what follows, I do not expect to show you that a high intake of sugar is the one and only cause of the diseases I mention. I do hope to persuade you, however, that, whatever your heredity, and however much you may persist in habits that are involved in producing one or another of these conditions, your chances of developing it would be significantly reduced if you reduced your sugar consumption.

Now what about evidence that a particular cause produces a particular disease? Broadly, there are two chief types of evidence, epidemiological and experimental. By *epidemiological*, I mean evidence that there is an association between the intensity of the supposed cause and the presence of the disease. Such evidence deals with this sort of question:

Is heart disease more common in populations that eat more sugar?

If there has been an increase in the number of people suffering from the disease, was there also an increase in the consumption of sugar?

In any one population, has any more sugar been eaten by the people that actually have the disease than by those who do not have it?

Experimental evidence is produced when you attempt to answer this sort of question:

Does the feeding of sugar to animals in a laboratory lead to heart disease?

Does the removal of sugar from the diet reduce the chances of animals or people getting heart disease?

You may also ask rather less direct questions, such as: short of producing the disease itself, does the feeding of sugar produce the kinds of change you normally find associated with the disease?

As to general laws, it seems to me that one or two biological principles ought especially to be remembered in these days of very rapid changes in our environment. First, living organisms can often adapt to a change if it is not too rapid or too profound. If, however, the change is very rapid and very profound, the organisms may succumb. It may be that in a population, some individuals will be more resistant and may survive even though the majority may die. If the change persists, a new population may ultimately arise from the survivors, in which all the individuals will be equipped with this higher resistance. It is likely that, for a fairly considerable alteration to occur in a population, something between 1,000 and 10,000 generations are needed. In human terms this would range anywhere from 30,000 to 300,000 years.

The second principle is less obvious, but I believe it is a logical corollary of the first. It is that, if there have been great changes in man's environment that occurred in a much shorter time than 30,000 years, there are likely to be signs that man has not fully adapted, and this will probably show itself as the presence of disease of one sort or another.

I know people tend to resent this thought, but I am convinced that you will not find an exception to this rule. Think again of cigarette smoking, which in America has increased from an average of twelve cigarettes per person per year in 1920 to seventy cigarettes a year in 1970. Think of the rapid decrease of physical activity: the use of labor-saving devices, the widespread use of the car, the television, and radio— all of these have made affluent man into an extraordinary sedentary animal during the past twenty or thirty years. And few today would deny that cigarette smoking is a potent cause of lung cancer and that both cigarette smoking and sedentariness are important causes of heart disease.

I could go on and point to the indisputable fact that every single new drug that has been introduced has sooner or later been shown to produce unintended bad effects as well as the intended good effects—though let me hasten to add that this is of little consequence if the good effects are important and the bad effects unimportant.

If, then, there is reason to be concerned about a dietary cause of a widespread disease, one should look for some constituent of man's diet that has been introduced recently, or has increased considerably recently. And by "recently" I mean over a short period in evolutionary terms. Conversely, a dietary constituent is unlikely to be the cause of a common disease if it has been a significant part of man's diet for a long time— say, one million years or more. If there is a constituent that is new or that now forms a much larger part of our diet than previously, one should also ask what has brought this about.

It is these considerations that should be borne in mind when one considers the total evidence that involves sugar consumption in the production of diseases in man. These considerations are so important that it is necessary to look at each of them rather more closely in order to understand their uses and limitations. This is what I propose now to do—not in very great detail, but sufficiently for you to understand why a great deal of what I write in this book has been the subject of argument and disagreement, and why I nevertheless believe that the total picture is fairly convincing.

First, then, *epidemiology*. The questions seemed reasonably straightforward: How much disease exists in different populations? How does it relate to sugar consumption? And so on. But in fact the questions are by no means easy to answer. Take the question of the prevalence of disease. To begin with, for most diseases there is no record anywhere of how many people suffer at any given time.

For example, no one knows how many people in America or England have a duodenal ulcer, or even what the prevalence of dental caries in these countries is. The diagnosis of duodenal ulcer, or the measurement of the precise amount of dental decay, is not easy and not sufficiently precise for all physicians to agree in every instance. And even if you were to hazard a guess as to the prevalence of duodenal ulcer or dental caries, by counting, for example, the number of cases treated in hospitals, you could not possibly find out the statistics for a country that lacks well-organized medical and dental services—and this applies to more than two-thirds of all countries in the world.

You might imagine the situation to be easier for those diseases that are often fatal, because you could then look at the record for mortality. But once more doctors do not always agree about a diagnosis of coronary thrombosis or particular sorts of cancer. The cause of death that different doctors report may therefore differ. Doctors in different countries tend to have different standards, and statistics from the less well-developed countries are again often quite unreliable.

Epidemiological studies also require a knowledge of food consumption—in this particular instance, a knowledge of sugar consumption. Now it so happens that it is easier to find out how much sugar is currently being eaten in a country than how much is consumed of any other food. In almost every country in the world, all sugar is produced in factories. Consequently, production, export, and import are well recorded. But even so, this information may not be sufficient for present purposes. It does not tell you how sugar is distributed through the population, and this it is most important to know.

Let me explain. Imagine two countries with exactly the same average consumption of sugar—suppose an average of sixty grams a day (about two ounces). Suppose that in one country most people eat about forty grams and relatively few eat over one hundred grams a day. In the second country, quite a number of people eat very little sugar indeed, but a large proportion eat over one hundred grams a day. If at least one hundred grams of sugar a day are necessary to produce coronary thrombosis, then more people would clearly be affected in the second country, even though the average for both countries is the same.

There is also the question of how long the disease takes to develop. It seems that coronary thrombosis and also diabetes show themselves only many years after their onset. Ideally, then, one wants to know people's sugar consumption over perhaps twenty, thirty, or forty years. It is clearly impossible to get this information. One can only hope that a careful measure of consumption today will, in many instances, give at least some idea of whether a person takes a lot of sugar, or a moderate amount, or little, and also whether he has maintained this habit for much of his life.

These, then, are some of the limitations of epidemiological evidence. One cannot, of course, ignore such evidence; the questions to be answered here are too important for us to discard any possible clues as to the cause of diseases such as coronary thrombosis. But you should constantly bear in mind the limitations of this type of evidence. Especially you should not be surprised if it seems less than conclusive; you may have to be content if it simply gives an idea about a possible cause that can then be followed up by research in other directions.

Under the heading of epidemiology, I also include evolutionary findings. Here the chief limitations are the uncertainty of some of the records. While most anthropological authorities take the view that man has been a meat-eater for several millions of years, they do not have an exact picture of what he ate and, especially, how much he ate of each food. The presence of large numbers of animal bones near human remains make it certain that he ate some meat, but it can be argued that meat was only a small part of his diet, that he ate mostly vegetable foods, and that these were bound to leave far less in the way of evidence than animal bones. This is not the place to argue the matter in detail, but I am in agreement with the majority who hold that primitive man was largely carnivorous.

All in all, epidemiological evidence does not provide conclusive proof of the relationship between diet and disease. It will, however, add important information to my case, and the total evidence will, I hope, be sufficient to convince you to the point that counts—the point "beyond reasonable doubt."

I now turn to the *experimental* evidence of what causes disease, the ways in which this evidence is gathered and the ways in which it can be legitimately interpreted.

One of the best ways to understand human disease is to reproduce the condition in rats or guinea pigs or other laboratory animals. By this means, medicine has gained a good understanding, though by no means yet complete, of such hormone diseases as excess or deficiency of the thyroid hormone or of the hormones of the pituitary gland or of the parathyroid glands. Again, most modern knowledge about nutrition—about calories and protein and vitamins and mineral elements—comes from work with laboratory animals.

On the other hand, when researchers can't produce a disease in animals, they are tremendously handicapped. There was a long delay before medicine found out how to treat pernicious anemia. This was because every suggested treatment had to be tried on patients with the disease. After very many years of hard research work, it was discovered that eating raw or lightly cooked liver was effective. Then, whenever a new extract from liver was made, it had to be tested in a patient with untreated pernicious anemia.

It was only after an interval of twenty-three years that this work ultimately resulted in the discovery that the active therapeutic agent in liver was vitamin B_{12}. There is no doubt that this long interval would have been very much reduced if the researchers could have been conducting the same tests on rats or rabbits or some other animals in the laboratory.

Coronary disease as it occurs in man has not been produced in any of the ordinary laboratory animals. There have been suggestions that it has been produced in some primates, but no one yet knows whether this can be done regularly and at will. In any event, it is going to be extremely difficult and costly to set up a laboratory with the hundreds of monkeys that would be necessary in order to carry out all the experiments needed to get somewhere near solving the problem of coronary disease.

What can be done more easily is to try and reproduce in the common laboratory animals as many as possible of the characteristics that are found to be commonly associated with the disease in man. The one characteristic that everyone has talked about for years is a raised level of blood cholesterol. It is widely accepted that the chances of someone's developing a heart attack are higher when blood cholesterol is higher. It is reasonable, then, to suppose that the experimental manipulation of the diet or of other conditions that raise the level of blood cholesterol in animals may be concerned with producing coronary disease in man. As everybody knows, there have been thousands of these sorts of experiments.

More difficult to produce than an increase in cholesterol are those changes in the arteries that are called "atherosclerosis," which I describe in a later chapter. Not all animals are equally susceptible to this condition. It is relatively easy to produce changes in the arteries of rabbits, but much more difficult in rats. And when one does produce fatty changes in the arteries, there is always the question as to whether they are the same as those that occur in human atherosclerosis. There was for a long time—and there is still in some minds—a doubt whether what is produced in the rabbit is really similar to the condition in man. Occasionally, enthusiastic research workers are carried away sufficiently to claim that they have produced experimental atherosclerosis when what they have really produced is something demonstrably and grossly different.

What one would like to see would be experiments that produce many of the characteristics of coronary thrombosis all together in the same animals by the same means. Still better, since it is not possible to produce coronary thrombosis itself, it would be good to see the same experiments carried out in several species of animals, so no one can be misled by some unusual response by one species that happens to be studied.

One ought also to take into account something of the normal habits of the animals. If, for example, one is studying the effects of diet, it does not seem to me to be sensible to include foods that are not normally part of the animal's diet or normally part of man's diet. The diets of herbivorous animals like the rabbit ordinarily contain very little fat and virtually no cholesterol. It is not surprising to me that diets that are high in fat and that contain cholesterol produce pathological changes in rabbits. I do not believe that this should be accepted as proof that similar diets will produce similar effects in carnivorous or omnivorous species of animals, including man, who have consumed such diets for hundreds of thousands of years.

One could also experiment with human beings, provided one could be sure that no harmful effects would be produced. The intention clearly would be not to produce coronary thrombosis but to produce temporarily the types of changes that are known to accompany the disease. Once again, the commonest change that has been looked for is an increase in the level of cholesterol in the blood.

Let me break off for a moment to make a point about the measurements research workers carry out when they perform experiments such as those I have been talking about. Of course a most important guiding principle is to measure the substances that, like cholesterol, are known to be considerably changed in concentration in the condition that is being examined. But research is often limited by the methods available for carrying out the measurements. It may be that for a particular substance either no method exists or none that is suitable for routine use, since it may require very special apparatus or may involve very laborious technique. Conversely, it may be that quite simple methods exist for measuring the substance, even though it may be—or turn out to be—that this is not quite so relevant to the disease that is being studied.

This, I believe, is the position with studies on coronary disease. If it is true—and I am still far from convinced—that the most important change in this condition is the increased level of some of the fatty materials in the blood, then there is a lot to be said for the view of many workers that levels of triglyceride (neutral fat) are more informative than are cholesterol levels. But while it has been quite easy for a long time to measure cholesterol in the blood, only in the last four or five years have there been simple methods for measuring triglycerides. Consequently there is a vast amount of information about the levels of cholesterol and what sorts of conditions change it, but so far very much less information of this sort about levels of triglyceride. And not everybody is convinced of the importance of cholesterol in heart disease. One distinguished American research physician has written that blood cholesterol is a biochemical measurement still in search of clinical significance!

One final sort of experimental evidence is to see what will cure or prevent the disease; from this, within reason, one can draw conclusions about the cause. An obvious example is scurvy, which is cured by giving oranges or lemons; it was this discovery that ultimately led to the identification of the cause of scurvy: a deficiency of vitamin C, which is contained in fruits and vegetables.

But there are two possible ways in which one can be misled—one obvious and one less obvious. The obvious one, though often overlooked, is that there are some conditions like the rheumatic diseases where the symptoms fluctuate. A period of pain is frequently followed by a period of remission, so that any treatment given while the disease is worrying the patient is likely to be thought to have produced the subsequent improvement.

One can also fall into a rather more subtle trap. I can best explain this by an example. Many older people who suffer from a variety of diseases gradually develop a degree of heart failure, and one of the effects is swollen legs due to dropsy (edema). This can be relieved if large amounts of vitamin C are taken, for the vitamin acts as a diuretic and increases the loss of fluid through the kidneys. Though this cures the symptoms of heart failure, the condition was clearly not due to a deficiency of vitamin C.

A more obvious example, if perhaps a rather ridiculous one, is that curing a headache with aspirin does not imply that the headache was caused by aspirin deficiency.

Let me here refer to the results of experiments on the effect of changing the diet in attempts to prevent coronary disease. Since these experiments have all been designed to test the effect of altering the fat content of the diet, and not the effect of altering the sugar content, it will be best to discuss these experiments at this point rather than later, when I shall be concentrating on the case against sugar. It is also useful to do this here because I shall be able to demonstrate another of the difficulties in research into the subject of diet and heart disease.

There have been about a dozen experiments, or trials, in which fat intake was changed by reducing the amount of saturated fats like butter fat and meat fat, and by adding a vegetable oil like corn oil. In most trials, the doctors studied people who had already had one or more attacks of coronary disease. The research workers tried to see whether the change of diet reduced the patients' chances of getting another attack compared with a similar group whose diet had not been changed.

This sort of study is called a "secondary prevention trial." The other sort of study is the "primary prevention trial," in which the investigators change the diet of apparently healthy men and see how many develop coronary disease, again compared with a matched group whose diet has not been changed.

Only three of the reported trials have been entirely of the primary-prevention sort, although one other trial is a mixture of primary and secondary because it studied people who had had a previous coronary attack as well as people who had not. Since it is now agreed that one is unlikely to get reliable results in a primary-prevention trial unless many thousands of subjects—perhaps as many as 60,000—are included, one can dismiss at least the first of the trials straightaway because the author studied only 265 subjects. A more quoted trial is that of the Anti-coronary Club of New York, although here, too, fewer than 1,000 people were studied. More importantly, however, many of the subjects dropped out during the trial, and there are several reasons to suppose that those who remained were no longer balanced by the control subjects. Moreover, the diet not only changed the amount and kind of fat, but reduced the amount of sugar and altered the total intake of food as well. If it turns out in the end that the diet really produced a reduction in the chances of people's dying from coronary disease, it will be impossible to know which of the dietary changes was responsible.

The third primary-prevention trial is still progressing in Finland and uses patients in two mental hospitals, each with about 200 patients. In one hospital the dietary fat was changed, and after six years it appears that the patients in this hospital had rather fewer heart attacks than the patients in the other hospital. It turns out, however, that there was about 40 percent less sugar in the diet of the healthier patients than there was in the diet of the patients in the other hospital.

I shall not go into detail about the other studies, except to say that they really are extremely difficult to run. Subjects tend to drop out; or one finds that the diets differ in other ways from those originally arranged; or the control subjects are not in fact exactly matched to the experimental subjects in spite of the original care that was applied in selecting them. All of these criticisms apply, for example, to the very elaborate and careful study by Drs. Seymour Dayton and Morton Lee Pearce in Chicago.

Suppose, however, in spite of the evidence to the contrary, it does in the end turn out that large amounts of unsaturated fats in the form of vegetable oils do reduce your chances of getting a heart attack. I would suggest that one should still be careful not to accept this as proof that heart disease is caused by a deficiency of the constituents of vegetable oils.

It could be that such an oil is acting in much the same way that vitamin C does in relieving dropsy, or that aspirin does in relieving headaches. You would think of this particularly if you were told that experiments have shown that both human beings and experimental animals require quite small amounts of these vegetable fats to keep them healthy in all the ways by which we have been accustomed to measure health.

Now you are told that, on the other hand, in order to prevent human beings from getting one sort of disease, they will have to take some twenty or thirty times the amount that was previously considered to be adequate. Let me point out that these amounts could not possibly have been provided in primitive human diets but depend on the fact that man now produces his own food, including sources of vegetable oils, and has the elaborate technology to extract and purify these oils for human consumption. Let me especially stress also that unnaturally large quantities of any substance, from all that research has shown up to now, are almost certain to cause unwanted side effects. There is already evidence that even moderate amounts of unsaturated fats, when given to babies, produce signs of mild deficiency of vitamin E, and there is also evidence that these fats may be involved in producing cancer in adults.

9

Tracking Down
Coronary Thrombosis,
the Modern Epidemic

No one today can be unaware of the tremendous concern about the large number of people dying from coronary heart disease. In America and Britain, they account for more than one-fifth of all deaths. In these and other affluent countries, at least one out of three men over the age of forty-five will die of heart disease. It is not surprising that a great deal has been written and discussed through books, magazines, radio and television programs about this problem over the past ten years. But I find that there is still such a lot of misunderstanding about what in fact heart disease is, that I had better clear the air with a few definitions and descriptions before going on to consider the causes.

I hope you don't think this is unnecessary. It may well be that you already have what you believe is a nice, simple picture of heart disease and how it comes about. If so, it probably goes like this:

There is a fatty material in blood called cholesterol. As you grow older, the amount in the blood increases, especially if you have food that contains too much meat fat or butter fat. Because of the high level of cholesterol in the blood, some of it tends to become deposited on the inside of the walls of the arteries, including the coronary arteries. Since these supply blood to the heart itself, their gradual narrowing by the deposited cholesterol reduces the blood supply to the heart, and you then get pain in the chest when you exercise—angina, or more correctly, angina pectoris.

The cholesterol deposits also encourage blood clots to form, so that sooner or later one or another coronary artery, or one of its branches, becomes completely blocked. As a result, the blood supply to a larger or smaller part of the heart is cut off, and then you have your heart attack—pain, unconsciousness if the heart stops, death if it does not soon start beating again.

This is what I call the *Reader's Digest* view of a coronary attack. And because it is oversimplified, it is sufficiently misleading for me to ask you to bear with me while I go through the story again in more detail, and more in keeping with the real events. I want especially to differentiate between what medicine *knows* is happening and what research is still uncertain about.

Like any other organ of the body, the heart can be affected by many different sorts of disease, so that strictly speaking it is as silly to speak of heart disease as it would be to speak of arm or leg disease. What people usually mean by heart disease is what is varyingly called coronary heart disease, or coronary thrombosis, or myocardial infarction, or ischemic heart disease. Even this statement, however, is rather misleading, because these conditions are not quite the same. You will understand the situation better if you try to follow the disease process as it affects the heart—insofar, that is, as science understands it. I say this because in many ways no one is as yet clear as to the development of the condition, or conditions.

In human terms almost everybody knows what I am discussing. One common picture is that of an individual, more usually a man than a woman, and most commonly over the age of sixty, who is often apparently quite healthy until he is stricken with a severe pain in the chest. He may fall unconscious and may not recover; or the pain may gradually diminish and he will be put to bed for some weeks. If he does recover from his first attack, he may have subsequent attacks after a shorter or a longer time, with again the chance that one of these will prove fatal. Sometimes the events are different. The picture then is of a person, again often apparently well, who dies so suddenly that he has virtually no time to complain of pain or of any other symptom.

The course of events leading to the established disease or diseases is unfortunately not at all clear. Indeed, whatever I now write, however carefully, will represent the views of many of the experts in this field, or even most of them, but there will always remain some who will disagree with some or all of the events as I outline them.

Let me begin by talking about the so-called "deposit" on the inside walls of the arteries. The deposit is called atheroma, the condition is called atheromatosis. The word *atheroma* is Greek for porridge, and refers to the patches of yellowish irregular material found on the inside of the walls of the arteries; these patches are sometimes called plaques.

No one is quite sure what starts the process. Many believe that it starts with an aggregation of blood platelets on or in the wall of an artery. The platelets are tiny discrete bodies in very large numbers, floating in the blood together with the red and the white blood corpuscles. When they stick together in this way, they encourage the formation of tiny blood clots. Around these clots there is gradually built up a mass of fatty material that includes a fairly high proportion of cholesterol. In due course, these patches become fibrous, much as scars form on a cut on the skin. It is the combination of atheroma and fibrous scars that leads to the eventually risky stage known as atherosclerosis. Later still, the plaques may degenerate and become chalky and hard.

Atherosclerosis can occur in arteries all over the body, although it is more likely to occur in some sites than in others. It probably starts at quite an early age, perhaps in the teens; according to some authorities, it starts even earlier. As it develops, it may begin to interfere with the flow of blood so that exercise may give you a pain in the chest because of narrowing of the coronary vessels (angina) or pain in the legs because of narrowing of the arteries to the legs (peripheral vascular disease).

In peripheral vascular disease, an increase in the extent of atherosclerosis leads to pain in the legs after you have walked for a shorter or longer distance. If the condition is not treated, there comes a time when the blood supply to the extremities is so diminished that a toe may begin to die of gangrene, or the whole foot, or even part of the lower leg. Treatment may consist of drugs that widen the arteries, or of operative procedures to improve the circulation by stripping the arteries of their atheromatous material.

In the heart, the coronary arteries may become increasingly blocked, resulting in more and more severe angina brought on by less and less effort. A more complete blocking may also occur, with or without previous angina. It could be that the blockage is due to a blood clot; this occurs more readily in an artery with atheromatous patches, partly because of the slow rate of flow in the blood and partly because the normally smooth interior of the artery now contains rough atheromatous material. But a block may also occur because the narrow coronary artery just goes into a spasm or contraction long enough to cut off the blood supply and cause a heart attack.

The outcome depends on several things. One is the size of the portion of the heart that was supplied by the artery before it became blocked. A second factor is the particular portion that loses its blood supply; some portions are very much more important in keeping the heart beating than are others. Thirdly, the outcome depends on whether the relevant section of the heart has blood vessels coming to it from a different direction, which can rapidly expand and bring enough blood to it through an alternative route.

If the affected section of the heart is small or relatively unimportant, the heart will stop for only a short time or not at all. If a portion of the heart has permanently lost its blood supply, that portion may die. This is called myocardial infarction and can be seen years later in the heart where the dead tissue has become replaced with scar tissue.

It seems that something quite different occurs in sudden death. It is probably also associated with severe atherosclerosis of the coronary arteries, but what appears to happen in this instance is that the heart stops beating normally and goes into a sort of very rapid shivering. This renders quite ineffective the heart's job of forcibly and regularly pumping blood round the body, and death ensues very rapidly indeed.

It is important to remember that it is possible to have quite extensive atherosclerosis without any symptoms at all. If so, it will be impossible to diagnose the condition unless some of the atheroma has proceeded to the extent of becoming chalky, so that it shows in an X-ray film. Most if not all adults in the well-off countries live with at least a fair degree of atheroma, but if they have no symptoms it is usually impossible to tell whether they do have atherosclerosis, and if so how much or where.

I hope you have not thought that this has nothing to do with the subject of this book. One of my main reasons for taking up research in this field was that I became more and more uneasy by the simplistic view of how people get coronary disease, the sort of *Reader's Digest* view I put forward before. This leads to the idea that the disease process is just a matter of cholesterol levels in the blood. This idea is now so firmly held by so very many people that they end up believing that anything that increases cholesterol in the blood is likely to cause coronary disease; that anything that reduces cholesterol helps to avoid the disease or even cure it; and that anything that does not invariably increase the cholesterol in the blood must have nothing whatever to do with the cause.

I know I am biased, but this picture—in my view a rather naïve picture—has held up considerably a proper understanding of the disease and its causes, and so a proper understanding of its prevention.

In fact, people with coronary disease are afflicted with very much more extensive disturbances than just a rise in the level of cholesterol in the blood. For one thing, there is a rise in other fatty components in the blood, especially the triglycerides, sometimes called neutral fats; many people believe this rise occurs much more frequently than does the rise in cholesterol. Secondly, other biochemical changes take place, including a disturbance of the metabolism of glucose or blood sugar in the same direction as that found in diabetes. There is often a rise in the level of insulin and other hormones in the blood, and sometimes a rise in uric acid. There are alterations in the activity of several enzymes. The behavior of the blood platelets is changed.

One could produce a list of at least twenty indicators that often register abnormally high, or abnormally low, in people that have severe atherosclerosis, and only one of these is the frequent though not at all universal rise in the level of cholesterol.

If you seek further evidence about the possible role of sugar or any other factor in producing heart disease in man, you should bear in mind the complexity of manifestations of the disease. This is particularly important in the sort of experiments my colleagues and I have conducted with laboratory animals. I shall talk about these in more detail in the next chapter.

The first proponent of the idea that diet could be a cause of coronary thrombosis, and since then its most vigorous defender, was Dr. Ancel Keys of Minneapolis. In 1953, he drew attention to the fact that there was a highly suggestive relationship between the intake of fat in six different countries and their death rates due to coronary disease. This was certainly one of the most important contributions made to the study of heart disease. It has been responsible for an avalanche of reports by other research workers throughout the world; it has changed the diets of hundreds of thousands of people; and has made huge sums of money for producers of foods that are incorporated into these special diets. As a result, too, a very great deal is now known about the effect of different diets upon the

processes of metabolism in the body, and especially
upon the processes of fat metabolism. And yet . . . there
is a sizable minority, of which I am one, that believes
that coronary disease is not largely due to fat in the
diet.

Let me start to argue the case by looking more
closely at the epidemiological evidence of the relationship between diet and coronary disease. From the beginning, a few people were a little uneasy about Dr.
Keys' evidence. Figures for coronary mortality and fat
consumption existed for many more countries than the
six referred to by Keys, and these other figures did not
seem to fit into the beautiful straight-line relationship
—the more fat, the more coronary disease—that was
evident when only the six selected countries were considered.

Also, evidence began to accumulate that not all fats
were the same; some seem to be good, some bad, some
neutral. At first, this was strenuously denied by Dr.
Keys, but by 1956 or so these differences were accepted
by him as they were by all other workers. The "bad"
fats were mostly animal fats such as those in meat and
dairy products (saturated fats). The "good" fats were
mostly vegetable oils (polyunsaturated fats). One example of "neutral" fats is olive oil (mostly a mono-
unsaturated fat).

It seemed appropriate, then, to look much more
closely at the figures of mortality and fat consumption
than had been done hitherto, and this I did in 1957.
By putting down all the information available from
international statistics, I found that there was a moderate but by no means excellent relationship between
fat consumption and coronary mortality, not even when
one separated the fats into animal and vegetable. A
better relationship turned out to exist between sugar

consumption and coronary mortality in a variety of countries. The best relationship of all existed between the rise in the number of reported coronary deaths in the U.K. and the rise in the number of radio and television sets (see diagram).

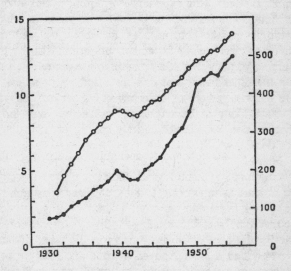

This table shows mortality due to coronary disease per 100,000 deaths (see line with heavy dots in chart) compared with the number of television and radio licenses per 1,000,000 population in the United Kingdom (see line with light dots in chart).

This last point serves two purposes, I think. The first and more superficial is to point to the possible dangers of finding an association between two events, and then saying that one event causes the other. It is unlikely, one would suppose, that your chances of becoming a coronary victim are increased just by the possession of television. But secondly, when you look more closely, this suggestion is not so stupid, after all.

The factors that have been implicated in causing coronary thrombosis include several that are associated with affluence—sedentariness, obesity, cigarette smoking, fat consumption, sugar consumption. On the one hand, therefore, the experience of coronary thrombosis in different countries will be higher in those in which there is greater affluence, as measured by such an index as cigarettes or fat consumption, but also by the number of television sets or automobiles or telephones. On the other hand, many of these indices of affluence are likewise indices of sedentariness. People who have TV are likely to be physically less active than those who do not. So it is not entirely silly to point to these relationships.

Here I was, then, in 1957, with information that international epidemiological studies suggested it would be at least as interesting to look at sugar consumption as to look at fat consumption. There was no suggestion at that time that the existing studies were a proof of the involvement of sugar. But, as in the story of fats, we now had a clue. And soon after my 1957 report, a Japanese research worker confirmed the relationship between sugar intake and coronary heart disease in twenty countries.

Apart from these general figures derived from international statistics, some studies exist of particular countries or populations. A British research worker demonstrated that the rise in coronary deaths in Britain very closely followed the rise in the consumption of sugar. In South Africa, it was shown that the black population had almost no coronary disease, while the white and the Indian population had as much as did the white population in America, Western Europe, and Australasia. It seems, however, that the situation is changing in South Africa: heart disease is beginning to occur also in the black population. These facts fit the figures for consumption of sugar, which has been high for a long time among whites and Indians; it was low among the black population until some eight or ten years ago, but it is now, with increasing affluence, rising rapidly.

In Israel, A. M. Cohen of Jerusalem found that recently arrived immigrants from the Yemen had very little coronary disease, though the disease was common among Yemenites who had immigrated twenty or so years earlier. Their diet in the Yemen had been quite high in animal fat and butter but low in sugar; when they arrived in Israel, they began to adopt the usual high-sugar diet of the country.

The Masai and the Sumburu are two tribes in East Africa that live very largely on milk and meat, so that they have a very high consumption of animal fat. There is, however, very little heart disease among them. You might say that this is because they are physically very active. Another possibility is that they have a different sort of metabolism from other people, and recent work suggests that this is actually the case for the Masai. It seems that they have a more efficient way of dealing with animal fat without being subjected to a rise in the level of blood cholesterol. It is not clear, however, whether this is some genetic characteristic of the Masai or whether they have become so good at metabolizing fats because they have been coping with large quantities all their lives.

But what is often left out of these discussions is that both the Masai and the Sumburu *eat virtually no sugar*.

Let me quote only one other special study, made in St. Helena. Coronary disease is quite common among these islanders. This is not because they eat a lot of fat; they eat less than the Americans or the British. It is not because they are physically inactive; St. Helena is extremely hilly, and there is very little mechanical transport. It is not because they smoke a lot; cigarette consumption is much lower than it is in most Western countries. There is only one reasonable cause of their high prevalence of coronary disease; the average sugar consumption in St. Helena is around one hundred pounds per person per year.

In summary one can say that in most of the affluent populations I have considered the prevalence of coronary disease is associated with the consumption of sugar. Since sugar consumption is only one of a number of indices of wealth, the same sort of association exists with fat consumption, cigarette smoking, cars, and so on. At this point, it would be equally justifiable to look at any one of these factors as being a possible cause of coronary disease.

You can also put this rather differently by considering the relationship between any two of the factors I have mentioned. If you look at how much fat and sugar is eaten in different countries, you find that they tend to be very similar for any one country; on the whole, both are low in poor countries, moderate in moderately well-off countries, and high in wealthy countries. You can say, if you wish, that fat is a cause of coronary disease, and the association between sugar and the disease is accidental because fat and sugar are related. Or you can put it the other way round, and say that sugar is a cause of coronary disease and it is the association with fat that is accidental.

When I arrived at this point it seemed to me that the next step was to look at the sugar consumption of individual people with and without coronary disease. For it is one thing to show that there is more coronary disease in countries where on the average more sugar is eaten, since averages can be so misleading. It is quite another thing to show that, in any one country, the man who eats more sugar stands a greater chance of getting the disease than the man who eats less sugar.

We devised what we thought would be a reasonably accurate way of getting at people's sugar intake, and measured this in twenty men with coronary disease, twenty-five with peripheral vascular disease, and twenty-five matched control patients (with other ailments) for comparison purposes. We spent a lot of time devising our method and choosing our subjects. The patients with coronary thrombosis, for example, were in the hospital with their first known attack; had up to this time no hint that they had heart disease; and had not consciously changed their diet.

We questioned them within the first three weeks after admission and asked about their normal diet before they were taken ill. We later showed that this method for measuring sugar intake was as good as the much more elaborate method normally used by nutritionists for other dietary constituents. We also showed that we were wise to have examined the diets of patients who had previously been apparently quite well. When we talked to them one or two years later, what they then called their normal sugar intake was in fact considerably lower than what they had reported on the first occasion.

In our study we found a very substantially higher sugar intake in patients with coronary disease and with peripheral vascular disease than we found in the control subjects. The median values were 113 grams a day for the coronary patients, 128 grams for the patients with vascular disease, and only 58 grams for the control patients.

When we published these results, there was a fair amount of criticism both as to our conclusions and as to our method. Much of this criticism we felt was not valid, but in one regard there was justification. We had assessed sugar intake in our subjects by asking each of them in person, in the hospital, about his diet. Because of this personal contact we knew which patients had arterial disease and which were control subjects. It was possible that we were unconsciously biased by this knowledge and might therefore perhaps have exaggerated the sugar intake of the arterial patients and minimized that of the control subjects. In order to overcome this objection, we simplified our dietary questionnaire so that each patient himself could fill it in. The questionnaires were handed out by the ward sisters, and only after we had calculated the diets did we enquire about the category the respondents belonged to.

The results of our second study were very similar to those of the first study. The median sugar intake in the coronary patients was 147 grams; in the control subjects—this time there were two groups—it was 67 grams and 74 grams.

Since that time, several other workers have examined the sugar intake of people with and without coronary disease. Some have confirmed our findings that coronary patients have been taking more sugar; some have not. There are, I think, several reasons for the negative results. First, people who have had a coronary attack are very likely to reduce their sugar intake, consciously or unconsciously, as we in fact found. You can just imagine what a shock it is to have had "a coronary" and how careful people will be to make sure they reduce their chances of getting another attack by keeping their weight down. The first thing people tend to do in this situation is to reduce their sugar.

Secondly, we made certain that our controls suffered from no sort of condition that might affect their diet. So we chose healthy workers in a factory, or other patients who were hospitalized because of, say, a broken leg but who had no systemic condition. Thirdly, we have found differences in sugar intake between different socio-economic groups and between different ages, so we made quite certain that our control subjects matched our arterial patients in these respects.

These are the sorts of reasons, I believe, why it is very possible that a less than careful selection of people to act as controls might lead to the false conclusion that there is little or no difference between the amount of sugar they eat and the amount eaten by people who develop coronary thrombosis.

It has, however, been said by my critics that, since not every investigator has found that individuals with coronary disease have been high sugar consumers, the sugar theory is entirely disproved. Most of these critics are, like Dr. Keys, strong supporters of the fat theory. The interesting point about this is that *no one* has ever shown any difference in *fat* consumption between people with and people without coronary disease, but this has in no way deterred Dr. Keys and his followers.

Let me here deal with another criticism by the same people. They say that sugar cannot possibly be a cause of heart disease because there has been a vast increase in the disease in the U.S. during the last forty or fifty years, while sugar consumption has remained almost unchanged during that time. But to say this is to misunderstand and misinterpret what you can reasonably expect from population studies. First, as I've said often,

I believe sugar is an important cause of heart disease but certainly not the *only* cause. Sedentariness and smoking are only two of the other causes that are involved, and both of these have considerably increased during the last half-century. Secondly, it takes a long time for sugar to produce its harmful effects, so that the high sugar consumption of the 1920s could have had its maximum effect only in the last decade or so. Thirdly, it could well be that a high sugar consumption is more harmful in young people than in older people. We saw earlier that there has been a great increase in the consumption of soft drinks, ice cream, cookies, and cakes; it is very largely the young people that take these foods. The middle-aged, on the other hand, have become increasingly figure-conscious, and many now have reduced their sugar intake. So it seems that the constancy of the *average* consumption of sugar hides an increased consumption in young people, and a decreased consumption in older people.

You will remember what I have now said several times in this book. The epidemiological evidence cannot by itself *prove* that sugar or any other factor is a cause of coronary disease. It can only provide clues as to possible causes. We can then look for the other kinds of evidence to see whether our theories make sense.

One more point. Since I have so often been accused of saying that sugar is *the* cause of coronary disease, let me repeat what in fact I have said or written every time I have discussed the problem. Several factors are concerned in the production of coronary disease. One is genetic, others are environmental. The genetic factor is responsible for some people being more susceptible to the environmental causes than others. Among the environmental causes are overweight, cigarette smoking, physical inactivity—and also a high intake of sugar.

It may turn out that they all ultimately have the same effect on metabolism and so produce coronary disease by the same mechanism. But this remains for further research to elucidate. In the meantime, we must expect to find some people who get a heart attack although they don't eat much sugar, and some who have not had a heart attack although they eat lots of sugar.

10

Eat Sugar and See What Happens

I shall now summarize some of the results we and others obtained in giving sugar-rich diets to experimental animals and to human volunteers.

Let me remind you that the basis of these experiments is to divide the human subjects (or the animals) into two groups, and give them diets that are as far as possible identical except for the type of carbohydrate they contain. In one group, the carbohydrate consists entirely or mostly of starch; in the other, it consists entirely or mostly of sugar. Some of the experiments that have been carried out are elaborations of this method; for example, in one experiment the animals were divided into four groups in order to vary the type or amount of fat as well as the type or amount of carbohydrate.

First, here are some results with rats. Consistently we find an increase in the level of triglyceride in the blood of male rats (see Diagram 1). The rise is proportional to the proportion of sugar we put into the diet. Often, though not always, we find an increase also in the level of blood cholesterol in male rats; we have not found a rise in cholesterol levels in female rats, although we have done fewer experiments with these than with males.

In addition to these experiments with normal diets, we have also used diets containing abnormal types of fats (see Diagram 2). By adding very saturated fats instead of the unsaturated fat that we usually use, and by adding a large amount of cholesterol to the diet, too, we have produced much higher levels of cholesterol and of triglyceride. When we substituted sugar for starch in these diets, there was a still greater rise in cholesterol and triglyceride.

DIAGRAM 1

Blood cholesterol and triglyceride levels (milligrams in 100 milliliters) in rats fed ordinary diets with and without sugar.

DIET	CHOLESTEROL	TRIGLYCERIDE
Without sugar	59	37
With sugar	61	53

DIAGRAM 2

Blood cholesterol and triglyceride levels (milligrams in 100 milliliters) in rats fed diets with cholesterol and saturated fat, with and without sugar.

DIET	CHOLESTEROL	TRIGLYCERIDE
Without sugar	577	144
With sugar	787	262

Sugar produces very many more changes in rats than increases of cholesterol and triglyceride. I do not know how many (and which) of these will be found to be related to changes that favor the development of atherosclerosis and coronary disease in man. But I shall mention a few of the effects of sugar that at present seem to be linked to these conditions. I shall discuss still other changes later on in connection with other conditions in man.

Many research workers have studied the mechanisms by which the body makes and stores fat; the idea is that factors affecting these mechanisms may have something to do with the fatty materials that constitute atheroma. Along these lines, our studies have included the measurement of some of the enzymes that are concerned in fat synthesis and storage. Our first measurements were of an enzyme in the liver called pyruvate kinase. This enzyme is important in the production of fat in the body from a variety of substances derived from the diet. An increase in activity is taken as a measure of the fat-forming activity of the liver, the major site of fat synthesis. Young rats given sugar in the diet showed, after ten days, five times as much enzyme activity as did rats without sugar.

Recently, we have been measuring the activity of an enzyme complex called fatty acid synthetase, which is closer to fat synthesis than is pyruvate kinase. It exists especially in the liver and in the fat tissue (adipose tissue). In the liver, an increased activity implies greater production of fat, which is then carried in the blood stream. In adipose tissue, an increased activity implies a greater removal of fat from the blood for storage.

With a sugar diet instead of a starch diet for thirty days, rats developed twice as much synthetase activity in the liver, and one-third as much in the adipose tissue. A rise in the liver and a fall in the adipose tissue suggests that more fat was put into the blood stream by the liver. Nevertheless, there was no compensatory increase in the enzyme that would be responsible for storing this in the adipose tissue; on the contrary, there was a decrease in the enzyme. We believe we have an explanation for this. It has to do with the fact that the hormone insulin is involved in converting the glucose part of sugar into fat but is not involved in converting fructose into fat. This now gets into very complicated biochemistry, so I shall not do more than say that this is an example of the complex actions of sugar that I shall take up in Chapter 15.

The changes in the enzyme that take place when you put sugar into the diet, and when you take it out, occur very quickly; in less than twenty-four hours, you can find the difference produced by the two diets, and if you then change the diets over, the enzyme activity is reversed, once more in less than twenty-four hours.

I mentioned earlier that coronary disease in man is associated with a number of features other than the levels of fatty substances in the blood. So we have looked for some of these features in our sugar-fed rats. The effects include a deterioration of the efficiency with which the body deals with high levels of blood glucose; a change in the properties of blood platelets; and a change in the level of insulin in the blood. Rats fed high-sugar diets for a few months show all of these features.

Given a dose of glucose on an empty stomach, rats on a normal diet show a moderate rise in the blood level, which rapidly returns to fasting level. Rats being kept on a high-sugar diet show a higher fasting level of blood glucose, a greater increase after the glucose dose, and a longer time before the level falls to fasting level. I shall have more to say about this behavior of glucose ("reduced glucose tolerance") when I discuss sugar and diabetes.

One cubic millimeter of blood contains about 250,000 of the small bodies called platelets; about 5½ million red blood corpuscles; and about 7,500 white blood corpuscles. If one cubic millimeter is an unfamiliar measurement, you can convert it into more familiar units by multiplying this by 65,000 to get the approximate numbers in one cubic inch, and by multiplying this again by 700 to get the approximate numbers in the body of an adult man.

The blood platelets are very much involved in the process of blood clotting. This is a highly complex process in which an important early step, or perhaps the very first step, is a change in the properties of the platelets; they become more sticky so that they can stick more readily to the walls of the arteries. They also clump together more readily.

These and other changes are common in people with severe atherosclerosis or coronary disease. We have recently tested the platelets of our sugar-fed rats, and found that they clump together (aggregate) distinctly more easily than do the platelets of the rats fed without sugar. The behavior of platelets is another matter that I shall bring up again later on.

I am increasingly inclined to believe that the most likely clue to an understanding of coronary disease will be found in a disturbance of the hormones of the body. This is why I think it important that Professor A. M. Cohen and others have shown that sugar-fed rats develop abnormalities in the special cells of the pancreas that produce insulin. Very recently, my colleagues and I have found that sugar-fed rats also develop enlarged adrenal glands.

We have not been successful in producing atheroma in our rats because the strain of animals we use is resistant to the disease. But other workers have been able to do so. In Paris, Dr. L. Chevillard and his co-workers have recently reported that rats develop atheroma of the main blood vessel, the aorta, when sugar is included in the diet.

Although atheroma did not develop in our rats, we analyzed the aorta to see if there was any difference in the fatty substances within the walls of this artery. We found substantially more cholesterol and triglyceride in the rats eating the sugar diet than in those eating the starch diet. We also looked at the effect of adding saturated fat or unsaturated fat to the diet, and found that they made no difference to the fatty substances in the aortic tissue.

I have been talking so far about our experiments with rats, since most of the experiments carried out by ourselves and by others on the effects of sucrose were done with these animals. However, some experiments with other animals have also been done. Rabbits fed sugar have been shown by us and by other research workers to develop a raised level of cholesterol. In cockerels and in pigs, we ourselves have found that sugar increased the level of triglyceride. Our pigs also developed a high level of insulin in the blood. Cockerels of the Rhode Island Light Sussex cross developed quite definite atheroma of the aorta with sugar, but not with starch. In a second experiment, with White Leghorn cockerels, we measured the area of the aortas that was affected by fatty deposits. It came to 46 percent of the aortas in the chickens that were fed the diet with sugar, and 1 percent in those of the chickens fed the diet without sugar.

What about human subjects? For the last eight years, Professor Ian Macdonald of Guy's Hospital in London has carried out many experiments with people who were given mixtures of food components, mostly for a few days, with and without sugar. Briefly, he has found that, in young men, sugar raises the level of cholesterol in the blood, and especially raises the level of triglycerides. This does not happen with young women. It does happen in older women, after the menopause.

Professor A. M. Cohen of Jerusalem has done experiments that for the most part lasted longer than those of Professor Macdonald, and his subjects were eating normal foods rather than mixtures of pure food items. They were given diets in which the carbohydrates were either mostly starch, in the form of foods like bread, or given fewer starchy but more sugar-rich foods. Professor Cohen and his co-workers found that the sugar diet produced a rise in cholesterol level, and also an impairment in glucose tolerance.

Our own experiments have usually involved carefully measuring the ordinary diets of young men and then getting them to replace part of the starch with sugar while making as few other changes as possible. We carried out extensive examinations on these men while they were on their normal diet; again at the end of two weeks on the high-sugar diet; and then two weeks after they had gone back to their ordinary diet.

In our first experiments with nineteen young men, the sugar-rich diet produced an increase in blood triglycerides in all of them after two weeks. In addition, six of them showed other changes; they put on about five pounds in weight; the level of insulin in the blood rose; and there was an increase in the stickiness of the platelets. All of these changes disappeared entirely, or almost entirely, two weeks after the men went back to their usual diet.

Three aspects of these results we found especially interesting. The first was the fact that a quarter or a third of our subjects showed this special sensitivity to sugar, while the remainder did not. This suggested to us the idea that only a proportion of men are susceptible to coronary thrombosis through eating sugar.

Secondly, the rise in the level of insulin recalled to us that there had been two or three British research workers who in the last four years have suggested that a raised level of insulin could be a key factor in the production of atherosclerosis.

Thirdly, we were intrigued that the men who were susceptible to sugar, as shown by the rise in insulin, also put on a lot of weight while on sugar, and lost it within two weeks after going back to their normal diet. This reminded us of the association between overweight and the liability to coronary thrombosis.

Our suggestion that only some people get atherosclerosis from eating a lot of sugar led us also to suggest that there should be a difference between middle-aged men who have the disease and those who do not. People with the disease should include those who experience an increase in insulin from eating sugar, and there should therefore exist a relationship between the amount of sugar they eat and the level of insulin. Those who by middle age have no sign at all of atherosclerosis will include those who are not susceptible to sugar, so that there should be no relationship between their sugar intake and the level of insulin.

We tested this hypothesis on two groups, each consisting of twenty-seven middle-aged men; one was a group of patients with peripheral vascular disease and the other a group of men with no symptoms who were coming to a clinic for a regular check-up. The results, plotted on a diagram, confirmed our prediction. On the whole, those patients who ate more sugar had higher insulin levels than did those who ate less sugar; among the "normal" people, those who ate more sugar had the same levels as those who ate less.

A second experiment with twenty-three men produced several of the same results, but also some additional features. Once again, after two weeks on the high-sugar diet, all of the men showed a rise in triglyceride, and six of them a rise in insulin and platelet stickiness. This time, however, all the men also showed a distinct rise in blood cholesterol, and an *improvement* in glucose tolerance. I shall have more to say later about this effect on glucose tolerance.

Curiously enough, these additional results were not caused by a higher sugar intake in this experiment compared with the last; in fact, the average daily sugar intake was 300 grams compared with an intake of 440 grams in the first experiment. We believe that the fact that we do not always find a particular change when we give a high sugar diet (for example, no increase in cholesterol levels in our first experiment but an increase in our second experiment) is due to the tremendous interaction of the changes produced by sugar, and the ability of the body to counteract some of these changes by adaptation of its metabolic processes. Amplification of this view I must also reserve for later discussion.

We asked those volunteers who had shown the rise in insulin and the other associated changes to help us with some additional experiments. In one of these experiments, we gave three of these men a high-sugar diet once more, and examined more closely the effects on the platelets; we also did the same with three of our volunteers in whom sugar had not produced a rise in insulin. We compared, that is, potential "hyperinsulin" people with "control" people.

What we did this time was to look at the behavior of the platelets when they were suspended in blood plasma and subjected to a high electrical potential. This procedure, called electrophoresis, causes the platelets to move toward the positive pole at a particular speed. When one now adds a very small quantity of a substance called adenosine diphosphate (ADP), they move very slightly more quickly; when one adds more ADP, the platelets move distinctly more quickly. At least, this is what happens with blood platelets from normal individuals.

Different behavior is seen with platelets from people with a variety of disease conditions, the most noticeable of which is atherosclerosis. Here, the platelets move much quicker in the electric field with the low concentration of ADP, and more slowly again when the concentration of ADP is increased.

You will understand, then, that we were interested to see what a sugar diet does to the platelets both of people in whom it produces an increase in insulin and of people in whom it does not. We found the answer quite quickly. When they were taking their usual diets, the platelets of the three hyperinsulin men and of the three control men behaved normally; however, after ten days on the high-sugar diet, the platelets of the hyperinsulin men took on the behavior of people with atherosclerosis, but the platelets of the control people did not change. A week after the high-sugar diet, the behavior of the platelets of the hyperinsulin men began to revert to normal.

Another experiment with our hyperinsulin volunteers was conducted to see whether another hormone, this time a hormone produced by the adrenal glands, was affected as well as insulin. We asked eleven of them once more to go on a high-sugar diet. Before they did so, and two weeks after they had begun, we measured both insulin and another hormone, cortisol, which is related to cortisone. We found that the insulin level in fasting blood increased by about 40 percent after two weeks on the high-sugar diet; the level of cortisol, however, increased very much more, to between 300 percent and 400 percent of the original value. This observation recalls our finding that sugar produces an enlargement of the adrenal glands in rats.

If our work is confirmed, we shall be able to "screen" people for their sensitivity to sugar. If a short period on a high-sugar diet produces a rise in insulin or cortisol, we shall know that they are in danger of developing coronary disease from eating too much sugar. If a high-sugar diet does not affect these hormones, then we shall know that sugar will not give them coronary disease, although of course it might still produce other ill-effects.

11

The Ill-Effect of Too Much (or Too Little) Blood Sugar

The way the body works is largely a matter of keeping the organs and tissues in a pretty constant environment inside the body. Anything, for example, that makes the level of sugar (glucose) in your blood fall below normal, or rise above normal, is promptly followed by actions that restore it to its original level. These actions are controlled partly by the nervous system but chiefly by the hormones. If for any reason the control mechanisms are not working properly, you will have an excessive amount of sugar in the blood, or a deficient amount, for part or all of the time. The condition of a high blood sugar is called hyperglycemia, and that of a low blood sugar, hypoglycemia.

SUGAR AS A CAUSE OF DIABETES

The commonest cause of hyperglycemia is diabetes. Diabetes (more strictly, diabetes mellitus) is a disease that has been studied in very great detail for quite a long time—certainly over one hundred years. Research workers are still, however, not at all clear about several features of the disease. In trying to summarize what is known, I shall inevitably have to make it sound much simpler than it really is; I shall have also to be more dogmatic than the limitations of current knowledge warrant.

Broadly speaking, diabetes occurs mostly in children or in middle-aged men and women. Juvenile diabetes tends to run in families rather more than does "maturity onset" diabetes. Again, when children with diabetes grow up, they are usually quite thin; maturity onset diabetes is most commonly found in overweight people. Soon after von Mering and Minkowski showed in 1890 that diabetes could be produced in a dog by the removal of its pancreas, it became evident that the groups of cells in the pancreas called the islets of Langerhans were responsible for producing a substance that prevented diabetes. Recently, the jubilee of the effective preparation of this substance by Banting and Best in 1921 was celebrated. The substance was given the appropriate name insulin (*insula* is the Latin word for island).

It was natural, then, to imagine that all cases of diabetes were caused by a failure of the islets of Langerhans to produce enough insulin. But it is now known that this is not always true. On the whole, such a failure is the more common cause of juvenile diabetes, but not of maturity onset diabetes. The latter condition is often due to an insensitivity of the cells of the body to insulin. Ordinarily, it seems, insulin enables the cells to utilize the glucose from the blood, which is their main source of fuel. If, however, the cells have become insensitive to insulin, the pancreas produces more and more insulin in order to counteract the insensitivity.

It was usual to treat all forms of diabetes with injections of insulin. Nowadays, however, it is more common to treat patients with maturity onset diabetes with drugs by mouth. These drugs mostly fall into two groups: those that increase insulin secretion by the pancreas, and those that seem to increase the sensitivity of the cells to the insulin that is already being secreted by the pancreas.

Even if they have been under quite good control, by insulin injections or by oral treatment, people with diabetes are likely after several years to develop a number of other conditions. Among these are diseases of the eyes—cataracts and retinitis—and diseases of the arteries—peripheral vascular disease and coronary thrombosis. No one quite understands why these complications arise, although it may be partly because of long-standing abnormal blood sugar levels, or because of other abnormal substances in the blood such as "ketone bodies."

As I shall show in Chapter 15, there is reason to believe that arterial disease may arise from a continuing high level of insulin. I shall then discuss the interesting association between diabetes, overweight, and arterial disease, and the fact that people with any of these conditions are likely to have excessive insulin in the blood.

There are several reasons why I believe that eating too much sugar is one of the reasons why people get diabetes—mostly maturity onset diabetes, but possibly juvenile diabetes, too. First, there is the epidemiological evidence. Much of it parallels what I have already cited for coronary thrombosis, but here the evidence is fraught with even more difficulties.

In some ways one could have expected an association between diabetes and sugar (or any other environmental factor) to be simpler than that for coronary thrombosis because diabetes is more readily diagnosed during life.

In fact, not many countries have the facilities for the large-scale and fairly elaborate surveys that would be needed to detect people who have diabetes. And as for mortality statistics, the difficulty is that people with diabetes often die of one or another of the many complications of the disease, and the death may then be certified as having been due to the complications rather than to the diabetes itself. So science is on rather uncertain ground about the prevalence of diabetes, and I can only give you the thoughts or views that are commonly, but not universally, held by the experts.

They believe that diabetes in the well-off countries is much more prevalent today than it used to be. If you look for it carefully, by seeing whether there is sugar (glucose) in the urine, or by testing the level of glucose in the blood, you can find at least mild diabetes in something like 2 percent of the population in Western countries. Currently, it is on the whole more prevalent in these countries than it is in the poorer countries. In some instances, such as among the people of Indian descent studied by Dr. G. D. Campbell in Natal, South Africa, there is a much higher prevalence than among their relatives still living in India. The average intake of sugar in Natal is said to be 110 pounds or more a year; in India, it is between 12 and 15 pounds a year.

Moreover, there is much more disease among the fairly wealthy Natal Indians than among the poorer. Dr. Campbell also points out that the village Zulus of South Africa have virtually no diabetes, while its prevalence among those living in the towns is almost as high as that in the white population. The amount of sugar consumed by the villagers was until relatively recently quite low, but has increased by more than ten-fold since the middle 1950s. It will be interesting to see whether there has been the increase in diabetes in the rural areas that Dr. Campbell predicted.

One other epidemiological study worth mentioning is that of Dr. E. Ziegler of Switzerland. He has compared the mortality due to diabetes in Switzerland with sugar intake, using a rather novel method of assessing this as "the sugar climate"; this is the total amount of sugar consumed over a period of years. He then demonstrated that the mortality due to diabetes over a period of twenty years, both in men and in women, is very highly correlated with the sugar climate.

The view that diabetes may be caused by eating sugar has long been held by many people. The name "sugar diabetes" of course refers to the fact that sugar (glucose) is found in the urine of affected persons. But people also take the name to refer to the cause of the disease as well as to one of its symptoms. Again, for more than one hundred years before insulin was discovered, it was known that diets low in carbohydrate and especially in sugar were the best way of treating diabetes.

Yet the first detailed epidemiological evidence, put forward by Professor (now Sir Harold) Himsworth some thirty-five years ago, suggested that the disease was associated most closely with fat consumption. He showed that the mortality from the disease in different countries was reasonably proportional to the average amounts of fat in their diets. But he himself expressed surprise that this was so, knowing that a diet high in fat was the accepted treatment for the disease.

Himsworth wrote:

The dietary factor which parallels these changes (in mortality and prevalence of diabetes) most closely is the consumption of fat, and this correlation is surprisingly consistent. . . . We are thus left with the paradox that, though the consumption of fat has no deleterious influence on sugar tolerance, and fat diets actually reduce the susceptibility of animals to diabetogenic agents, the incidence of human diabetes is correlated with the amount of fat consumed.

Looking at the problem again some twenty-five years later, I wondered whether Himsworth's difficulty arose from making the common assumption that all carbohydrate was equal. Since total carbohydrate consumption is similar in most countries, there was no reason to suspect carbohydrate as a cause of diabetes. But when you consider the different forms of carbohydrate, then you find that the prevalence of diabetes is related better to the amount of dietary sugar than it is to dietary fat. This is especially true if you take into account the probability that it may take twenty years or so for the diet to produce diabetes, as Dr. Campbell suggests.

When I related the number of people dying of diabetes in different countries with the amount of sugar or fat that was eaten some twenty years earlier, I found a high correlation with sugar and no correlation with fat. The sort of relationship with fat that is sometimes found, and was found by Himsworth, comes about because, as I pointed out, average fat consumption in different countries is fairly well related to their sugar consumption. The most likely explanation of the situation, then, is that sugar intake is a cause of diabetes, and fat intake is only secondarily related to diabetes through its association with sugar intake.

A year before I made these observations, a very interesting paper appeared from Professor A. M. Cohen in Israel. He examined people for the presence of diabetes, and his study was especially interesting for two reasons. First, it was made on Jews, who are said to have more diabetes than non-Jews. Secondly, he was able to compare people of four different backgrounds: from Western Europe and America; from North Africa; from the Yemen (people who had recently arrived in Israel); and from the Yemen (people who had arrived twenty or more years earlier).

All but the recent immigrants from the Yemen had a similar prevalence of diabetes. But the recent Yemen immigrants had a prevalence of 0.06 percent compared with 2.9 percent for the earlier Yemen immigrants. Later, Cohen and his colleagues showed, as I mentioned in relation to his study on heart disease, that the major change in the diet of the Yemenites in Israel was a great increase in sugar consumption; there was very little change in their fat intake.

In addition to these epidemiological studies, there is also experimental evidence that sugar may produce diabetes. Again, some of the early studies were those of Professor Cohen, and my colleagues and I have confirmed his results. Rats fed with sugar developed a decreased glucose tolerance resembling the condition seen in diabetes. That is, when a dose of sugar is given by mouth to a fasted animal, the already abnormally high level of glucose increases to a still more abnormal level, and it does not return to the fasting level within the usual one and one-half to two hours.

Cohen showed that this impairment of glucose tolerance occurred in rats after three weeks or so when there was 67 percent sugar in the diet; after six weeks when it contained 40 percent of sugar; and after about thirteen weeks with 33 percent sugar. The glucose tolerance recovered after a few days on the normal diet. When sugar feeding was resumed, it deteriorated again, but this time only after a few days.

It looks as if the secretion of insulin by the pancreas had been permanently impaired, at least in part. This is in conformity with the general biological observation that the effect of continuing stimulation of a tissue is first to improve its activity; but ultimately it may result in exhaustion.

Later, Professor Cohen worked for a few months in my department, and again we studied the effects of feeding sugar to rats. This time, we injected tolbutamide, one of the drugs used in the treatment of diabetes. This stimulates the pancreas to secrete insulin, so that it lowers the blood glucose level. We argued that, if the pancreas had been damaged by the sugar diet, tolbutamide would not be able to call forth as much insulin, and the blood glucose would not fall so much.

This is just what we found. After eight weeks, the injection lowered the blood glucose in one experiment by 31 percent in the starch-fed rats, and by 26 percent in the sugar-fed rats. In a second experiment, the figures were 32 percent and 27 percent.

In human subjects, a high-sugar diet maintained for several weeks has been shown to reduce sugar tolerance, and a low-sugar diet for several weeks has been shown to improve it. We ourselves measured glucose tolerance in the experiment with young men that I described earlier, where they were fed a high-sucrose diet for two weeks.

In the first of these experiments, we found no change. In the second experiment, we found an improvement in glucose tolerance after one week, and a slight reversion toward the normal after the second week. This may seem strange; in fact, it is not at all surprising.

The first effect of the sugar would be to stimulate the pancreas so that it becomes more efficient in producing insulin; this is a period of adaptation. But if you go on giving a high-sucrose diet, the pancreas eventually begins to get worn out, as it were; this is the period of exhaustion. So the improvement in glucose tolerance that we showed after one week would not contradict the deterioration that people found after several weeks. Nor would there be a conflict in the fact that we found no change in our first experiment; we might very well have made our measurements at a point where developing deterioration just about cancels out the initial improvements induced by the sugar.

Finally, I should mention the relationship between diabetes and coronary disease. The relationship goes both ways, as it were. On the one hand, if you are a diabetic you have a higher than normal chance of suffering from coronary disease. On the other hand, if you have coronary disease you have a higher than normal chance of developing diabetes—or at least an impaired glucose tolerance that is sometimes called "preclinical diabetes." I believe this sort of overlap is important when you come to try to understand how sugar can be involved in causing these two diseases, a question that I shall attempt to answer in Chapter 15.

HYPOGLYCEMIA

The people who know this condition best are diabetics. Sooner or later, they run into the situation of having taken too much insulin, or too much of one of the new oral drugs, and they get the most uncomfortable symptoms of hypoglycemia, sometimes leading to unconsciousness. But hypoglycemia also occurs in many people who are not diabetics, although they rarely get it so severely as to become unconscious.

You begin by feeling hungry and weak, and you may begin to sweat. You may then start shaking, feel faint and dizzy, and start a severe headache. If the condition persists, you might get mentally confused, stagger about, and speak indistinctly or nonsensically. At this point, you might even be arrested for being drunk and disorderly.

All these symptoms arise because your blood glucose has fallen to an abnormally low level. It is easy to understand the situation when it happens in a diabetic. He may have taken his insulin or pill, which lowers his blood sugar, and then not have had his normal breakfast because of some interruption. It is also easy to understand how it occurs in the rare circumstances when a patient has a tumor of the pancreas causing an overgrowth of its insulin-making cells.

The way it happens in other people is almost certainly because of the consumption of a lot of carbohydrates, especially sugar. The effect of eating any meal is to increase the level of blood sugar. If sugar or starch or glucose is in the meal, then all or part of it turns up in the blood quite quickly as glucose. If protein or fat is in the meal, then their digestion products, too, will in part be converted into glucose, but more slowly.

The rise in blood glucose is only temporary, because one of its effects is to stimulate the pancreas to produce more insulin. This causes both an increase in the breakdown of the blood glucose and an increase in its conversion into glycogen to be stored in the muscles and liver. As a result, the level of glucose falls back toward normal.

A more than normally rapid absorption of a great deal of glucose occurs if a lot of sugar is consumed, especially if it is taken between meals when there are no other food constituents in the stomach that might delay absorption. There is then a rapid rise of blood glucose, and an excessive amount of insulin is secreted. Because of this, the subsequent fall of blood glucose is excessive, the level becomes abnormally low, and if it is low enough symptoms of hypoglycemia will appear.

There is some evidence, too, that continued high intake of sugar can, at least for a time, result in an increased sensitivity of the pancreas, so that it responds more readily still by an increased secretion of insulin, and hypoglycemia becomes even more likely.

How then do you treat hypoglycemia? Well, if you don't bother to think out the consequences of what I have just said, then clearly you treat a person with low blood sugar by giving him sugar. And the effect is pretty miraculous; within a few minutes, all the sweating and weakness and dizziness disappear. But now think back for a moment and you will see that this, however effective, is in the long run just what you don't want to do.

What you must do is to prevent the large swing in blood glucose that each time ends in an excessive fall. You want to eat foods that result in a gentle rise in blood sugar, so that you don't evoke an excessive output of insulin by the pancreas. That is why the best treatment for bouts of having too little sugar in the blood is the paradoxical treatment of avoiding sugar in your diet as much as possible.

Finally, let me say a word about hypoglycemia in babies. Premature babies sometimes suffer from hypoglycemia, presumably because their hormonal control of the level of blood glucose has not yet become properly balanced. This can be quite serious, and premature babies have been known to become unconscious or even die from hypoglycemia. Because this is an acute and hazardous situation, the best treatment is to give them sugar (sucrose) or, still better, to give them glucose by mouth or even intravenously.

Babies who are not born prematurely, one would

imagine, would not develop hypoglycemia so readily but might still be expected to be rather more sensitive to the damaging effect of sugar than adults. When you consider how soon babies are given sugar, and how much, it is perhaps not so surprising that there appears to be an increase in the number of babies who develop hypoglycemia when they are a few months old.

12

How Sugar Can
Give You a Pain
in the Middle

It was almost by accident that I began to become interested in the relationship between sugar and severe indigestion or dyspepsia.

I have been involved in the study of obesity and in its treatment for a long time. For a number of theoretical reasons, I began about twenty years ago to treat people with diets restricted in carbohydrate. At first, these diets were restricted *mostly* in carbohydrate, but also somewhat restricted in fat. After two or three years, however, I began to realize that it was necessary deliberately to restrict only carbohydrate, because it turned out in practice that if you do this, you automatically restrict your fat.* For a long time now, I have recommended this diet to all the very many overweight

---

*The low-carbohydrate diet I recommend is sometimes called the high-fat diet because people are told they can eat as much fat as they like so long as they cut down their carbohydrate. They then imagine that "as much fat as you like" is an enormous amount of fat. But when my colleagues and I actually measured what they ate, we found that they ate either the same amount of fat as before or a little less.

The diet is fully described in my book *This Slimming Business*, which was first published in Britain in 1958. It says you can eat as

patients I have seen, in the hospital or in my university.

As always, the interviews with these people begin with general questions about health, including as always questions about indigestion: "Do you have indigestion or any sort of pain or discomfort after meals? Where do you have the pain? What sort of pain is it? How often do you have it? How long does it last? What do you take to relieve it?"

There are lots of other questions about their health, of course, and then the patients are examined and weighed and measured. After a few weeks of repeated visits by the patient, I go back to these questions, and often find that, with loss of weight, they are not so short of breath, not so tired, have no pains in their hip joints, and their ankles no longer swell at the end of the day.

All these changes I expect, but what I did notice many years ago was that many of them said, with surprise, that my questions reminded them that they had stopped having indigestion. And this relief was observed not just after they had lost weight but almost from the moment they had begun the low-carbohydrate diet.

Let me interpose my personal experience. I have suffered from severe dyspepsia for most of my life, and was diagnosed some twenty-five years ago as having a duodenal ulcer. I was given what was then very up-to-date advice; I was told not to have an operation unless it became imperative; to continue with my work; to "take it easy" and not get too exhausted; and to avoid

much as you like of meat, fish, eggs, leafy vegetables, cheese, butter, margarine, cream, or any oil or fat. It recommends that you take up to half a pound of fruit a day and one pint of milk. It then gives you a list of the carbohydrate content of foods and drinks in units of five grams, which I called "Carbohydrate Units," and it tells you to take about ten of these in a day. To find out what can make up ten units (fifty grams) of carbohydrates, consult your physician or any source listing carbohydrate values of various foods.

spicy foods, eat more frequently, and eat small meals. I gradually gave up cakes and pastries too, because I found I always got heartburn after these foods. But I still had quite frequently to take antacid preparations such as magnesia or aluminum trisilicate.

I then discovered that, like so many very sedentary middle-aged men, I was beginning to put on weight. Obviously, I now reduced my carbohydrate intake very considerably, and this got my weight under control. Suddenly, a few months later, I became aware that my indigestion had almost entirely disappeared.

On the strength of these observations, I decided to set up a proper test of the idea that the low-carbohydrate diet does really relieve the symptoms of indigestion. This was a more formidable undertaking than you might think.

Severe indigestion often occurs in people who are under a great deal of stress and who are not always very reliable in their statements. Secondly, indigestion often comes in bouts—a few weeks of pain, and then, for no apparent reason, a few weeks or even months with no pain at all. If you happen to be taking some treatment—any sort of treatment—before you have one of these intermissions, then you are likely to believe that it was the treatment that made you better. Third, no doctor has a certain and objective measure of how much pain other people are experiencing; you have to accept their own estimate of whether their indigestion is better or worse, and, if so, whether it is slightly or considerably better or worse.

I did think it was worth trying, and so we set up a fairly comprehensive scheme of experiments that would eliminate these difficulties, or at least minimize them. The tests were carried out at King's College Hospital in London. Physicians and surgeons were asked to send us anyone coming to them complaining of severe dyspepsia that had lasted, though perhaps not continuously, for more than six months. Many had had symptoms for five years or more. The only patients who were not included in our experiment were those who were going to have an operation for their condition.

Each patient was carefully questioned and examined by a physician, and then sent on to a nutritionist. Alternate patients were carefully instructed either in the conventional dietary treatment now current, or in the low-carbohydrate diet. The conventional treatment consists of telling the patient to avoid fried foods and irritating foods such as pickles or foods containing spices, to take frequent small meals, and to avoid alcohol, especially on an empty stomach. At frequent intervals, each patient came back to the physician for assessment of the progress of his condition, and to the nutritionist to check the diet that he was following. The physician did not know which diet each patient was on; the nutritionist did not know how the patients were progressing.

After three months, the diets of the patients were reversed, so that those taking the conventional diet were transferred to the low-carbohydrate diet, and those taking the low-carbohydrate diet transferred to the conventional diet. The experiment was then continued for a further three months.

Having made the conditions of the experiment so stringent, we were not surprised that it took us more than two years to get together information on forty-one patients who had reported regularly for six months, and had, as best we could judge, adhered to our instructions. From the detailed records kept by the physician, he and I then separately assessed their total progress, and classified them as having shown no change, or having reported various degrees of improvement or deterioration at the end of each three-month period. Our assessment differed in only one or two instances in the degree of change, but not once did we disagree as to whether the patient reported that he was better or worse or just the same.

In summary, the results are pretty clear. Of the forty-one patients in our trial, two said that they were worse on the low-carbohydrate diet, eleven said that they were no different on either diet, but a decided majority—twenty-eight—said they were very much better on the low-carbohydrate diet. Some of these made it quite clear that the improvement was so great that nothing on earth was going to make them give up the low-carbohydrate diet.

One patient said, "I feel better than I have for five years." Another said, "I have never felt better round my stomach in all my life." The patients included men and women, some with gastric or duodenal ulcer, some with hiatus hernia, and some who probably had ulcers that, as so often happens, were not revealed by X-ray examination.

These results, of course, pleased us a great deal. They suggested that chronic and severe indigestion, from several causes, could be greatly relieved by diet alone in something like 70 percent of patients. This result was especially pleasing because there had been increasing disappointment in the last few years over the results of dietary treatment of this condition. Several research workers had put patients on fairly strict "gastric diets"—steamed fish, white meat, mashed potatoes, milk puddings—or on the more liberal but still fairly conventional diet I described earlier. All these investigators concluded that the diets did not seem to relieve the severe dyspepsia of their patients, whether or not they had definite ulcer.

Now it can no longer be said that diet does not relieve severe dyspepsia. The right diet will; only the wrong diet will not.

We believe that we now know at least one reason why people get dyspepsia, and why the low-carbohydrate diet works. This is that sugar irritates the lining of the upper alimentary canal—the oesophagus, stomach, and duodenum—and that the low-carbohydrate diet contains little sugar.

In a later chapter, I shall try to bring together the ways in which I think sugar produces its effects, including the effects on the digestive system. But let me here refer to one recent experiment that shows what sugar can do in the stomach.

Working with young men, we managed to persuade seven of them to swallow a gastric tube first thing in the morning. They did this before and again after two weeks of a high-sugar diet. Through this tube, we obtained samples of their gastric juices at rest, and then at fifteen-minute intervals after they had swallowed a bland "test meal" consisting mainly of pectin. Each sample was analyzed in the standard ways, notably by measuring the degree of acidity and digestive activity.

The results showed that two weeks of a sugar-rich diet causes an increase in both acidity and digestive activity of the gastric juice, the sort of change you often find in people with such conditions as gastric or duodenal ulcer. The sugar-rich diet increased the acidity by 20 percent or so; the enzyme activity was increased nearly three-fold. And let us remember that these effects were seen early in the morning, before breakfast, so that the high-sugar diet had made the gastric mucous membrane much more sensitive to the very mild stimulus of the pectin test meal.

Severe and chronic indigestion is a common symptom of an inflamed gall bladder (cholecystitis), usually associated with gall stones (cholelithiasis). Although we have not specially studied patients with gall bladder disease, it turned out that one of the patients included in our study of indigestion was, during the course of the study, diagnosed as having gall stones rather than inflammation of the stomach or duodenum. She was one of those whose symptoms cleared up almost entirely when she changed to the low-carbohydrate diet.

This is not very strong evidence about the involvement of sugar in producing gall bladder disease. And there is also not much experimental evidence, especially since we are not sure of the relationship between the human disease and the gall stones that can sometimes be produced in laboratory animals. Nevertheless, it is a fact that gall stones have been observed both in hamsters and in dogs that have been given diets containing sugar.

Patients with disease of the gall bladder are almost always put on a diet that is low in fat. Many physicians have found this fairly ineffective, but I am certain it would be worthwhile to conduct a carefully controlled trial of a low-sugar diet for these patients, along the lines of our trial with chronic dyspepsia.

13

The Eyes, Teeth, Skin, Joints—and Cancer

I now want to talk of a number of quite unrelated conditions in which there is evidence of very varying strength that sugar might perhaps be involved.

DAMAGE TO THE EYES

Opthalmologists had for a very long time wondered whether nutrition could affect the way the eye developed, and thereby affect such conditions as far-sightedness or near-sightedness. About thirty years ago there was some suggestion that near-sightedness (myopia) occurred in children when their diets were short of protein. The research on which this notion was based was not considered acceptable by the experts, and there is nowadays no support for this view. One of my colleagues, together with an ophthalmologist, looked at the problem by doing some experiments with rats. They too could find no effects of diets that were simply deficient in protein.

They then studied the effects of diets that were low in protein but also high in sugar, the types of diets known to be common among the rapidly increasing populations of large cities in poorer parts of the world. In one experiment, they fed rats on diets low in protein and with or without sugar. After six or seven months, both of these groups had grown poorly compared with control rats fed the normal high-protein diet. The investigators found no significant difference in refraction between the normal rats and those on the low-protein high-starch diet, but the rats fed the low-protein high-sugar diets had a considerable degree of myopia, amounting to one diopter.

In a second experiment, they took another three groups of rats: one group was placed on a normal diet; the second on the low-protein diet with sugar; the third group on the normal diet with the amount restricted so that rats grew at the same low rate as did the rats on the sugar diet. After nine weeks, there was no difference in refraction between the groups. But by fifteen weeks, the sugar-fed rats had developed myopia, again to the extent of nearly one diopter, compared with the normal group and with the poorly fed group.

At this point the diets of the second and third groups were reversed. One result was that the poorly fed group, with normal refraction up to the time of the change, became myopic within three weeks of starting on the diet with sugar. The other result was that the sugar-fed group with myopia at the time of the change-over did not improve during the whole of the rest of the experiment, even though it lasted for twenty-three weeks after the change.

We have also measured eye refraction in student volunteers who were the subjects of our most recent experiment. As before, we took a large number of measurements before and after they were given a high-sugar diet. After two weeks on this diet, there was a small but quite significant change in their refraction—but this time it was a change toward far-sightedness, not toward myopia or near-sightedness.

At present, we are suggesting that the reasons have to do with the level of glucose in the blood. Doctors have known for some time that diabetics develop a mild but noticeable degree of near-sightedness if their blood sugar is not properly controlled and, consequently, rises to an unduly high level. We believe that this may be the cause of the myopia occurring after a long period in our rats on the high-sugar diet; we know that such animals become mildy diabetic with a high blood sugar and that a low-protein diet probably accentuates the condition. In our students, the two weeks on a high-sugar diet tends to produce a low blood sugar, as I have shown, so that here one would have expected not myopia but far-sightedness.

As far as I know, only one other experiment has been reported on the effect of dietary sugar on the eye. This is some recent work by Professor Cohen of Jerusalem. This time he was working with researchers who were adept at using a very delicate technique that permits you to measure the electrical response of the retina when a light is momentarily flashed onto it. Again, Cohen compared two groups of rats, one fed a starch diet and the other a sugar diet.

After three months, the research workers tested the animals with the electroretinograph. They found an abnormally poor response in the sugar-fed rats. They drew attention to the fact that earlier work by Professor Cohen and others had supported the view that sugar is involved in producing diabetes, that diabetes often leads to severe retinal disease, and that this may well be preceded by much smaller defects such as those shown by the electroretinograph.

DAMAGE TO THE TEETH

Each year, millions of teeth are extracted by dentists from children all over the Western world. In the U.K. alone the loss is 4 million teeth, weighing more than 4 tons. In one survey in Dundee, Scotland, thirteen-year-old boys and girls were found to have an average of ten decayed teeth. More than one-third of British adults over sixteen have had *every one* of their teeth extracted.

The evidence from fossil man suggested that the condition now known as dental caries, or dental decay, occurred hardly at all in prehistoric times, before the introduction of agriculture and the great increase of starchy foods like cereals in man's diet. The disease became common only recently. There is no doubt that this is associated with the introduction of sugar as an increasing component of the conventional diet.

To understand the process of dental decay, it is necessary to know a little about the structure of the tooth. It is mainly made up of dentine, a sort of tough bone. This is covered by a thin layer consisting of enamel, the hardest tissue in the body. Inside the dentine is the soft pulp from which the dentine is made, and in it are blood vessels. As anyone who has had a toothache or visited the dentist knows, the pulp also contains highly sensitive nerve endings.

Dental decay begins from plaques of material that

stick on the surface of the teeth, and are found especially in the normal fissures and crevices of the tooth surface. The plaque is made up of a background material of protein and carbohydrate, which retains particles of food, debris from the saliva, and countless bacteria.

Present evidence is that dental decay proceeds by the production of acid by bacteria in the plaque, especially bacteria belonging to the type called *Lactobacillus acidophilus*. The acid is produced in the plaque as it adheres to the surface of the tooth. It is not washed away by the saliva but gradually attacks the dentine until, unchecked, it exposes the sensitive pulp. The production of acid is facilitated by the build-up of a complex carbohydrate in the plaque.

It seems that what the acid-producing bacteria like best in the plaque is the particular complex carbohydrate called dextran. This can be built up from any sugar, chiefly by other sorts of bacteria called streptococci, but very much more is produced from sucrose.

People differ in their susceptibility to caries; some are less susceptible partly because they appear to have inherited a higher resistance than normal, partly because they live where the drinking water contains adequate amounts of protective fluoride, partly because they clean their teeth frequently, but chiefly because they do not consume food and drinks that allow their teeth to come into prolonged contact with sugar. One day perhaps we shall be able to immunize people against the several sorts of bacteria that are involved in producing caries; at the moment it seems that everyone harbors the organism in his mouth.

The epidemiological evidence about the development of dental decay includes what I summarized earlier in regard to primitive man. I showed that carbohydrates in general are a relatively recent addition to man's diet. Perhaps the earliest specific mention of the association between sugar and caries was that of a German traveler who in 1598 remarked on the black teeth of Queen Elizabeth of England, "A defect the English seem subject to from their too great use of sugar." Much earlier, Aristotle spoke of teeth being damaged by figs, but he was not aware that their sweetness was largely due to the same sucrose that was later extracted from the cane and manufactured into the sweetmeats that ruined Queen Elizabeth's teeth.

Dental caries had become the scourge of the wealthier countries mostly during the present century. In the poorer countries it is now increasing quite fast and is already common among the wealthier sections of their populations. Several isolated groups until recently had little caries but have developed the disease rapidly after first coming into contact with Western foods; notable examples are the Eskimos and the inhabitants of Tristan da Cunha. Again, dental caries in children became less common in Western Europe during and soon after the two world wars, when sugar was scarce; its prevalence increased rapidly when sugar became freely available again.

These observations do not prove that sugar is a cause of dental decay. I have already pointed out that the association of disease and diet in different populations can only be viewed as a clue to the cause. Next one must see whether the individuals in any one population that get caries are those who eat a lot of sugar. Curiously enough, not much research of this sort has yet been done. The groups of dentists in Dundee to who I referred earlier examined thirteen-year-old boys and girls in 1960, 1961, and 1962. They found more dental caries in those who ate more sweets, but surprisingly they found no difference in caries among those who did and those who did not brush their teeth regularly.

Our own research, carried out in 1967 but on a much smaller number of children, also showed that there was more decay in children taking more sugar in solid foods (that is, more sweets, cookies, and so on). But we also found that this relationship between sugar and decay occurred only in children who did not clean their teeth regularly; if they did clean their teeth regularly, they few caries even when they ate a lot of sugary foods.

Many experiments have been done, especially in animals, to see what changes in diet affect the teeth. As always, the precise results differ according to what animals were used; exactly what the experimental diets were; how the diets were given; and for how long. The general results, however, seem clear. When there is no carbohydrate, little or no caries is produced. Diets containing starch or bread, brown or white, produce either the same amount of caries or a very little more. Diets with any sort of sugar produce much more caries, and the most "cariogenic" sugar is sucrose.

The best-known experiments with children are those done by the British Medical Research Council in 1950, and that done in Vipeholm in Sweden a few years later. The first study lasted for two years and showed that the addition of sugar during meal times had not increased the amount of caries in children. The second study compared sugar given in different ways for four years, and found that few additional caries occurred if the sugar was taken at meals, but much more occurred when it was taken as sweets between meals, and especially if it was taken as sticky toffees between meals.

Obviously, what matters is whether the sugar is in contact with the teeth for some time. Sticky candies and cakes and cookies between meals are the chief culprits, especially if they are allowed to remain without being exposed to a good and prolonged tooth-brushing.

During the past few years, a great deal of attention has been directed toward what is called rampant caries. Increasingly, babies are given pacifiers to suck that have a small container in which the mother puts syrup. The effect of this, or of giving ordinary pacifiers constantly dipped into sugar, is that the babies' teeth become rotten as they erupt, so that at the age of two or three years their mouths are full of blackened stumps. In one recent survey, one baby in twelve was found to be suffering from rampant caries; in another, the figure was one in eight.

One of the most interesting and unexpected of the observations of the role of sugar in producing dental caries comes from a study of a rare disease, hereditary fructose intolerance. Only a few families have been discovered with members suffering from this disease, and they become violently sick whenever they get fructose, or sucrose, which you'll recall is a compound made up of equal amounts of glucose and fructose.

Very early in life, therefore, they learn to avoid fruit and anything containing sucrose. They can and do eat starchy foods, since starch is digested to give entirely glucose. But even though they eat lots of white bread, made from what people like to call "refined flour," they have very little caries and what they do have is of a very minor degree.

DAMAGE TO THE SKIN

In measuring the amount of sugar consumed by
hospital patients, I was chiefly interested in those with
coronary disease. But it occurred to me that it would
be interesting to see how much sugar was taken by
patients with two or three other conditions. There are,
for example, conditions such as acne (blackheads),
which occurs quite frequently in teenagers, and which
many doctors believe is caused, or made worse, by
candy.

We measured sugar intake in these patients, and
compared it with that of people of the same age and
sex without acne. We also decided to look at another
common skin disease called seborrhoeic dermatitis, but
this time not because diet had been indicated by physicians. The reason was that this condition has to do
with the secretion of the glands in the skin of the oily
substance that is called sebum. There is some evidence
that this material is altered when the diet is rich in
sugar. So we measured sugar intake of patients with
this disease, too, and compared it with that of people
without seborrhoeic dermatitis, each one chosen so as to
be the same sex and age of a patient with the disease.

It turned out that the acne patients were not consuming any more sugar than the control subjects, but
that those with seborrhoeic dermatitis were taking appreciably more.

The implication of these results is that sugar is not
involved in producing acne, but may be involved in
producing seborrhoeic dermatitis. We could extend
these conclusions by saying that it is unlikely that acne

patients would get better if they ate less sugar, although it may be that they are especially sensitive. They might therefore be suffering from acne even though they do not take more sugar than other people, and if this is so they will indeed be better off by taking less sugar. But no one has really done a properly controlled test to see whether less sugar does make them better.

As for seborrhoeic dermatitis, the fact that they are high-sugar eaters at once suggests that we should see if we can improve them with a low-sugar diet. This we are now doing, and although the results are promising, we are not yet satisfied that we have studied enough cases to be certain.

DAMAGE TO THE JOINTS

Gout has always interested doctors. The popular idea of gout is that it is found in people who over-indulge in rich food and in alcohol; in England, we think of the retired colonel drinking his bottle of port a day. It is often thought to be very rare nowadays, but in fact it is not all that rare. It occurs mostly in middle age and later, and more in men than in women.

The reasons that made it seem worthwhile to look at the sugar consumption of gouty patients were pretty flimsy, I must admit. First, one of the features often found in people with atherosclerosis, and found in almost all people with gout, is a raised level of uric acid in the blood. Secondly, some Italian research workers have shown that the ingestion of fructose, which, you will remember, accounts for half of the digestion products of sugar, causes an increase in the level of uric acid in the blood. Thirdly, there is some indication that peo-

ple with gout are rather more likely to get atherosclerosis than are other people, and conversely that people
with atherosclerosis are more likely to have gout.

So we have been studying patients in two or three
rheumatism clinics. While we were mostly interested in
those that had gout, we also looked at patients with
another rheumatic disease, rheumatoid arthritis. Here
we did not have even a flimsy reason for looking at their
sugar consumption. We did it simply because we
thought that it might act as a sort of additional control
to the usual control subjects matched for age and sex
whom we were using for comparison with our gout
patients.

As we half expected, the patients with rheumatoid
arthritis were eating the same amounts of sugar as control subjects. But the patients with gout were taking appreciably more sugar than the control subjects; the
median values were 102 grams of sugar a day for the
gouty patients and 54 grams for the control subjects.

IS THERE A LINK BETWEEN SUGAR AND CANCER?

There are some cancers that appear to have become
more common in the last forty or fifty years, and that
also appear to be more common in the affluent countries
than they are in the poorer countries. So I thought it
might be worthwhile just to see whether there was any
relationship between the numbers dying from these
cancers in several countries, and the amount of sugar
that their population consumed.

The usual snags faced us with the epidemiological
studies. How many countries are there that keep proper
records of the causes of death in their populations?

Even where records are kept, how sure can you be that the diagnosis of cancer is correctly made, or made on exactly the same criteria, in different countries?

Some sorts of cancer can be diagnosed fairly readily; others are often mis-diagnosed. Because of this, we confined our attention to three or four countries where the experts tell me that there is a reasonably good chance of correct diagnosis. If a high sugar intake does play a part in producing some sorts of cancer, it would almost certainly do so after a pretty long period, during which the sugar consumption in the country as a whole, as well as the sugar intake of individual people, might have changed. But it is not unreasonable to assume that different people on the whole tend to like sugar in varying degrees, so that there would be a tendency for a man or woman either to eat rather a little, or to eat rather a lot, consistently over many years.

The evidence at present comes entirely from a study of international statistics and takes the form of an association between the average sugar consumption in different countries, and the experience of two or three particular forms of cancer. The best way of demonstrating this association is by the use of correlation coefficients. I have already mentioned this concept once or twice, but I have not explained what it is. Let me do so now.

On the whole, the taller people are, the more they weigh. It is all very well to say that there is "on the whole" this association between height and weight. But it would be better if we could say how close this association is. Suppose that it were a precise and absolute association, so that one person who was only a little taller than another would inevitably be heavier, and one still taller would be still heavier. If this were so, you would say that the correlation coefficient was 1.0.

Suppose, on the other hand, and this is even more unlikely, that there was no relationship whatever between height and weight, so that it would be just as likely for a five-feet-tall man as for a six-feet-tall man to weigh 150 pounds. In this case, the correlation coefficient would be 0. In fact there *is* a relationship, but not a precise one; tall people *tend* to be heavier, but that is all. If you work it out for adult men, the correlation coefficient between height and weight comes to about 0.6.

The figures I quote are from a preliminary attempt to look at the correlation between cancer and sugar consumption; we have to get more information and continue to examine the statistics. The correlation coefficients we have found so far are as follows:

Cancer of the rectum in men	0.60
Cancer of the rectum in women	0.50
Cancer of the breast	0.63

We also found high correlation coefficients for leukemia, although this is one of the conditions where diagnosis is less reliable. They were:

Leukemia in men	0.53
Leukemia in women	0.51

As I have said several times, I do not claim that we have proved that sugar can increase your chances of getting cancer. I do claim, however, that the relationships we have shown warrant a much more extensive examination of the possible role of sugar in this disease.

This is a very mixed collection of diseases, to be sure —cancer, dental caries, near-sightedness and far-sightedness, dermatitis, and gout. And the evidence that they are caused in part by an excessive consumption of sugar is by no means equally convincing for all of them. At one extreme, it seems that everybody is certain about the role of sugar in dental caries, except perhaps the manufacturers of cookies and candy. At the other extreme, there is as yet not much evidence that cancer of the rectum or of the breast is really very more likely to appear in people that eat a lot of sugar. I shall, however, be content if you will agree that in cancer especially, but also in gout and seborrhoeic dermatitis and refraction errors of the eye, it is worthwhile to pursue research to test the possible role of sugar in producing these conditions.

14

Does Sugar Accelerate the Life Process—and Death, Too?

SUGAR'S EFFECT ON GROWTH

Laboratory animals that are used to test diets are invariably weighed regularly, at least once a week. Almost everyone, therefore, who has looked at the effects of feeding sugar has obtained information about what this does to the rate at which the animals gain (or lose) weight. Sometimes an experiment also measures how much food the animals eat; in this way, research workers may be able to show that animals utilize their food with varying efficiency—eating the same amount on different diets, for instance, but gaining less weight with one diet than with another. Sometimes, too, but much less frequently, they not only weigh the animals but actually determine the composition of the body. By measuring how much fat and how much lean an animal has in its body, the research workers may find two diets that seem to result in the same gain of weight, but yield a different proportion of fat and lean.

Most workers have reported that sugar-rich diets

result in a slower gain in weight in young rats, young chickens, and young pigs. When they have measured the amount of food the animals eat, it often turns out that those on the sugar diet gain less weight for each one hundred grams of food. And when they have looked at the composition of the bodies of the animals, they sometimes find that there is more fat, and sometimes they find less.

Here are some examples. Male rats fed for six months from the age of six weeks weighed about 410 grams when we fed them without sugar; with sugar, they weighed only about 380 grams. The effect was more noticeable when the diets were rather low in protein; the rats then reached a weight of 320 grams when they had no sugar but 270 grams when they had sugar. In an earlier experiment with chickens, some American workers showed that sugar had no effect on the weight when protein was adequate, but did reduce the weight gain when the protein was not quite adequate.

Now what about the human animal? The evidence that sugar affects the growth of children is indirect. The work with animals suggests that a diet low in protein may be even more deficient when it is accompanied by sugar. It seems that the usefulness of a given amount of protein—its value in promoting growth—is diminished when sugar is present in the diet. While there is no direct evidence that what is true of growing children is equally true of rats and chickens, this interrelationship could be of particular interest in poorer countries.

One of the characteristics of such countries is the enormous increase in urbanization. There is a tremendous influx of people from the country into the big cities of India, Thailand, Ghana, Nigeria, and similar

countries, particularly in South America. The chief
effect on the diets is an increase in the consumption of
manufactured foods such as cakes and cookies and soft
drinks, so that the new arrivals, mostly extremely poor,
take even less protein but take more sugar. If the
effect in children is similar to that in young animals, the
combination of sugar and low protein would explain
even better the high incidence of protein deficiency than
would the low protein alone. This results in the dreaded
disease kwashiorkor that is so common, and so often
fatal, in children in the developing countries.

But a high intake of sugar is more usually an ac-
companiment of diets in well-off countries, and these
are more likely to be adequately supplied with protein
and usually with other nutrients too. The question has
been raised whether this high intake of sugar causes an
increase in growth, rather than a decrease.

The most active and enthusiastic proponent of this
idea is Dr. Eugen Ziegler of Switzerland. In a number
of remarkably detailed and forcefully argued publica-
tions, he has in the last six years drawn attention to
statistics from many countries of birth weight, of height
and weight of children, and of adult height. According
to the information he quotes, these measurements are
closely related to the amount of sugar in the diet.

Here are some of his examples. The birth weight of
babies in Basle, Switzerland, increased from an average
of 3.1 kilograms to 3.3 kilograms between the years
1900 and 1960, except that they were lower during
the periods of the two world wars; these changes
parallel the changes in sugar consumption. In Oslo, the
height of girls between eight and fourteen years old increased between 1920 and 1950; for fourteen-year-old
girls, the increase was more than four inches. The only

break in the increase was during World War II. Again, these changes in height were parallel to the changes in sugar consumption. Also in Norway, the height of adult men increased by about three-quarters of an inch between 1835 and 1870; and by another one and one-half inches between 1870 and 1930. The average sugar intake increased from 2¼ pounds in 1835 to 11 pounds in 1875 and to 67 pounds in 1937; current consumption is over 90 pounds, an increase of 40-fold over a period of about 130 years.

So far, I have mentioned the effect of sugar only on the height and weight gain in children, or of weight in experimental animals. Analysis of the bodies of the experimental animals often shows changes in the amount of fat, as I have said, and also changes in the size and composition of some of the organs. In our experiments with rats, we have mostly found a moderate decrease in the amount of body fat; in one experiment, from 35 percent of the dry weight of the animal to 30 percent. On the other hand, some workers have shown an increase in body fat—in baboons, for example. This is probably no real contradiction. There is reason to believe that the exact effect of sugar depends on the species of animals you study or even on the particular strain of such species as rats. It also depends on the age when sugar feeding begins, on whether you are studying male or female animals, and on how long the experiment continues.

The organs that have mostly been examined are the livers and the kidneys of experimental animals; these are extremely active in the body and are the organs that are first examined if you want to decide whether, for example, a proposed food additive is likely to be harmful. The effect of sugar is to produce an increase in the size of both the liver and the kidneys after a few days. This could have been due to an increase in size of each of the cells that make up these organs, or an increase in the number of cells. The latter seems the less likely, even though it is well known that the cells of the liver, particularly, can divide quite rapidly.

My colleagues have measured the number of cells in rats fed with starch and sugar by chemical determination of the amount of DNA in a given weight of liver. To our surprise and concern, they found that the increase was due only partly to an increase in the size of the cells; there was also a distinct increase in the number of cells.

The increases in weight of the liver that I have been talking about occur quite rapidly. More slowly, the liver of sugar-fed rats also accumulates fat, sometimes to a quite remarkable extent. Usually the increase is moderate; in one experiment, it increased from 7.4 percent of the dry weight to 9.2 percent. But when the diet was also deficient in protein, we had much larger increases in liver fat: from 18 percent to 46 percent for example. In chickens, we have also had very large increases in liver weight and in liver fat, even on diets with normal amounts of protein.

That sugar can produce fatty livers was in fact shown some thirty years ago in experiments by Sir Charles Best, one of the discoverers of insulin. He was looking at the effects of alcohol in producing fatty liver in rats, and demonstrated that this could be prevented if one of the B vitamins, choline, was supplied in adequate amounts at the same time. These results are of great importance, and frequently quoted. But he also showed that sugar had the same effect on the liver as does alcohol. This discovery, however, has been largely overlooked.

SUGAR'S EFFECT ON
MATURITY

One of the characteristics of affluent countries is the nutritional state of their babies and young children. There is nothing like the incidence of nutritional deficiency that one used to see—the pinched, starved, rickety children that were common in the larger cities. Instead, there is an appreciable number of fat children, many of them beginning to acquire, even well before they are a year old, the condition that will later turn into years of struggle against fat.

One of the characteristics of these overweight babies and children is that their growth in height is accelerated as well, and they tend to reach maturity early. Although few detailed statistics exist, it is agreed that obesity occurs in bottle-fed babies much more commonly than in the breast-fed. A recent paper in the British medical journal *Lancet* suggested that this happens because of the early introduction of mixed feeding, especially cereals. What is overlooked is that the usual formula for the bottle-fed baby is a powder consisting of, or largely based on, dried cow's milk to which ordinary sugar is added. It is also common practice to add sugar to the cereal feed when it is begun, and indeed quite common to add sugar to other foods as they are introduced, even to egg dishes and chopped meat and vegetables. Many of the canned baby foods that are now so commonly used also contain added sugar, and this applies not only to the desserts but also to many meat and cheese meals.

All this points to the possible role of sugar in producing childhood obesity. But there is now evidence that sugar may also produce other effects in children. One of the very remarkable changes that has occurred in human physiology during the last century is the reduction in the age when boys and girls reach maturity. Because it is easier to detect maturity in girls than in boys (by the date when menstruation begins), more information exists about girls; but studies also show the same change in boys.

Briefly, each decade has seen a decrease of some three or four months in the age at which puberty begins. In the past 120 years, the age at which Norwegian girls have reached puberty has fallen by almost exactly four years, from an average of seventeen years to an average of thirteen years. The same trends can be seen in Sweden, England, and the United States. In 1905, the average age of puberty in American girls was fourteen years and three months; today, it is just about twelve years. Incidentally, it is quite wrong to think that puberty occurs early in the tropics; it occurs, in fact, much later than it does in the better-off countries in temperate climates.

The usual explanation of earlier maturation is that it is caused by better nutrition in the wealthier countries, and by fewer attacks during childhood from infections and other diseases. But Dr. Ziegler has suggested, with a wealth of statistics, that the main cause is an increase in sugar intake. He believes that earlier sexual maturity is part of the total acceleration of growth that sugar induces. Although he has no experimental evidence, he produces a very plausible explanation in terms of the probable effects of sugar on hormonal secretion. I shall discuss this later in some detail.

In our own experimental work, we have made three observations that support the suggestion that sugar results in early sex maturity. When treating cockerels with sugar diets, we have noticed that their combs become red and enlarged earlier than do those of cockerels fed diets without sugar. At the end of one of our experiments, we found that the testes were distinctly larger in the cockerels fed sugar. With pigs, those receiving sugar were seen to be sexually more active, as shown by their frequent attempts to mount one another in the pen. In rats, sugar produces a distinct increase in the size of the adrenal glands, which, among other actions, produce hormones affecting sex development.

In support of Dr. Ziegler's finding is a report by Dr. O. Schaeffer of Canada. The particular interest of this study is that there has been a large increase in sugar consumption among the Eskimos in the Canadian north. Dr. Schaeffer studied Eskimos in three areas and measured birth weights as well as the heights and weights of adults and children at various ages. In one of the areas, the average annual sugar consumption had increased from 26 pounds to 104 pounds in eight years; in a second area from 83 pounds to 111 pounds in one year; and in a third area from 46 pounds to 61 pounds over five years. Birth weights increased in all of these areas—a small increase with the smallest rise in sugar consumption, and a larger increase, amounting to between one-half pound and one pound in one year, in the other areas.

Between 1938 and 1968, the stature of adult men increased by nearly two inches, and that of women by just over one inch. The height of the children increased much more. Boys and girls aged two to ten years were two inches to three inches taller; boys of eleven were four and one-half inches taller, and girls of twelve or thirteen were as much as eight inches taller. The latter change was accompanied by a lower age at which there was the rapid weight gain associated with puberty; in

1968, this occurred between the ages of eleven and one-half and thirteen, while in 1938 it had occurred between the ages of thirteen and one-half and fifteen. The Eskimos appear to show an advance of puberty similar to that which had occurred in Western Europe and America, but perhaps even more rapid.

The increased growth of children, and especially the earlier development of puberty, is generally assumed to be due to an improvement in nutrition, notably an increase in the intake of protein. This was the explanation given for the considerable increase in the growth of Japanese school children between 1946 and 1955. In fact, however, while the intake of animal protein doubled, the intake of total protein was only 10 percent more, and there is little evidence that the children measured in 1946 were deficient in protein.

The role of protein is even less likely when you consider that the intake among the Eskimos had in fact fallen from over 300 grams a day to just over 100 grams a day during the period that Dr. Schaeffer studied. There was also a substantial fall in the protein intake of Icelanders, one of the groups studied by Dr. Ziegler. On the other hand, in all these three examples —the Japanese, the Eskimos, and the Icelanders—the acceleration of growth was associated with a great rise in sugar intake.

SUGAR'S EFFECT ON LONGEVITY

Most of our experiments with animals were carried out for a relatively short time, and began with animals that were quite young, often only a few weeks old. We have had little experience of our own, therefore, in gauging the effects of different diets on the life span of rats, or cockerels, or pigs, or rabbits. We did, however, keep one simple experiment going much longer than usual, beginning with twenty-eight rats one month old. Of these, fourteen were given a diet without sugar and fourteen a diet with sugar. At the end of two years, we had eight rats alive in the starch group and only three alive in the sugar group.

More careful observations have been made by two other groups of research workers. One group in Holland fed some rats with a mixture of foods representing the average Dutch diet, and compared them with other rats that were fed the same mixture but with twice as much sugar. I should add that the sugar in the Dutch diet supplies about 15.5 percent of their calories, slightly less than the 16 percent or so in the average American diet and the 18 percent or so in the British diet.

Of the male rats, those fed the standard diet survived an average of 566 days; those fed extra sugar an average of 486 days. The survival time for female rats was 607 days as against 582 days. If the same proportional reduction in life span occurred in human beings, the extra sugar would result in the reduction of the Biblical "three score years and ten" to about sixty years for men and to sixty-seven years for women. The greater resistance of the female animals to sugar is another matter I shall discuss later.

The second study on longevity was carried out by some American workers from the United States Department of Agriculture. The diets were made up so as to contain either starch or sugar as the carbohydrate component. The investigators studied two strains of rats and, as I have mentioned, found that the strains responded differently to diets containing sugar. One lived just as long with either sugar or starch, although the sugar produced larger livers containing more fat. The other strains also had larger livers with more fat when they were fed sugar. In addition, however, their kidneys were also enlarged, and the rats died substantially earlier, at 444 days instead of the 595 days of the starch-fed rats. If you again calculate the longer survival as equivalent to seventy years for a human being, the life span with a sugar-rich diet was reduced to the equivalent of fifty-one years.

There is no evidence now that sugar affects the life span of human beings. But in the light of this animal research, it would not be an entirely absurd suggestion. One keeps hearing how much healthier people are now in the wealthy countries because of improvements in nutrition and in the reduction of infectious disease. As a result, it is reported, the average expectation of life has risen from about forty years a century ago to about seventy years now. But the former low average expectation of life was due largely to a high mortality in babies and young children; once people reached the age of twenty-five or so, they were likely to survive to almost the same age as Westerners do now. This is in spite of all the advances in nutrition and medicine and hygiene, so that it is reasonable to suppose that these improvements in health have at least partly been offset by some deterioration that holds back what otherwise might have been at least a slight, but very real, increase in life span.

That sugar might affect growth, maturation, and longevity is astonishing only if one continues to believe that all dietary carbohydrates have the same metabolic effect once they have been digested and absorbed. It not only ceases to be astonishing but becomes highly plausible, when one remembers that sugar can induce sizable alterations in the levels of potent hormones.

15

How Does Sugar Produce Its Effects?

One reason why many people are skeptical about the suggestion that sugar is bad for health is precisely that the number of illnesses in which I feel sugar plays a part is so large. When my colleagues and I say that so many conditions can largely be avoided or improved by avoiding sugar, it looks as if we have joined the panacea-mongers.

Take apple cider vinegar, the food cultists say, or brewers yeast with yoghurt, or wheat-germ oil, and you will stay young and healthy forever—well, nearly forever. Avoid sugar, *I* say, and you are less likely to become fat, run into nutritional deficiency, have a heart attack, get diabetes or dental decay or a duodenal ulcer, and perhaps you also reduce your chances of getting gout, dermatitis, and some forms of cancer, and in general increase your life span.

It is difficult, certainly, to imagine that the omission of one single food can produce all these benefits, or that its inclusion in the diet can be responsible, at least in part, for so many disparate diseases. Yet I do not believe that my suggestion is in the least implausible. As I have shown, sugar has a wide range of properties that

157

make it a popular constituent of foods and drinks; it is this versatility that is responsible for its use in so many commodities, and contributes toward today's high intake of sugar.

Because of these very varied properties, it becomes more plausible to imagine that sugar can produce such a large and varied number of effects in the body. But research workers are not at all sure of the mechanisms by which every one of the effects can be brought about. Much of what follows, therefore, is inevitably theoretical, but it will, I hope, at least serve the purpose of suggesting some of the lines along which further research can be done.

Sugar can be expected to produce its effects in three different ways. First, it can act locally on the tissues in the mouth or stomach before it is absorbed. Secondly, it can act after it has been digested and absorbed into the blood stream. Thirdly, it might possibly act by changing the types of microbes that live in the intestines. This could result in a change in the microbial products that appear and get absorbed into the blood, and these in turn might affect the body's metabolism.

The evidence that sugar produces all these actions varies from near certainty to highly imaginative speculation, but I think all of it is worth looking at. Even the speculative will serve a purpose if it leads to research designed to elucidate some of the remarkable properties of sugar in the body.

LOCAL ACTION

The link between sugar and dental disease

Fairly solid evidence exists, as I have already mentioned, about the ways sugar is involved in causing dental decay. The bacteria found in the mouth are stimulated to grow and to produce acid by most carbohydrates—by starch and by any sugars that are found in our food. Sucrose, however, is a particularly potent cause of caries for two reasons. First, sucrose is the main ingredient that results in particular foods' being sticky and adhering to the teeth; cookies and hard candies are notable examples. This in itself would be conducive to caries production, because the carbohydrate they contain is not washed away; as a result, the acid produced by bacterial action comes into prolonged contact with the tooth surface. But secondly, sucrose, unlike other carbohydrates, has the unique property of being readily built up into a material called dextran, which serves as a most effective raw material for the acid-producing bacteria.

The link between sugar and dyspepsia

The patients whom we treated in the experiment mentioned in Chapter 12 were suffering from a variety of conditions, including hiatus hernia, duodenal ulcer, or severe dyspepsia with or without actual ulceration. There is at present a great deal of discussion about the causes of these conditions. But I think we can explain why sugar can produce or exacerbate an inflamed mucous membrane in the oesophagus or stomach; why a low-sugar diet relieves the symptoms; and perhaps even why sugar can actually produce an ulcer in the duodenum.

If you think about the "natural" diet of man, by which I mean the diet before the beginning of agriculture, you will see that the constituents of his food would not be irritating to his stomach. This is because they do not have a high osmotic pressure.

(Let me explain what osmotic pressure is. It is a

property of a solution that is measured by its tendency to absorb more water to itself in particular conditions. If, for example, you put a strong sugar solution on fruit, the fruit will shrink because its moisture is, as it were, sucked out by the sugar. Or if you pour sugar on a cut in your finger, it will hurt as it does when you put salt on it, though not so much because salt has an even higher osmotic pressure than sugar. This again is because the cells of the skin shrivel by having to give up some of their water.

The osmotic pressure depends on the concentration of particles [molecules or ions] in the solution. If you are dealing with a material like starch, which has very large molecules, then even a strong solution will not have much osmotic pressure because it will contain relatively few molecules. On the other hand, a similar concentration of sugar will have a high osmotic pressure because the molecules are small and so there will be very many more of them.)

The diet of pre-Neolithic man, as I indicated earlier, contained lots of protein, a moderate amount of fat, and a little starch and sugar. Both protein and starch have large molecules, and fat doesn't dissolve in water at all. So the osmotic pressure would depend mostly on the small amount of sugar in this diet and the very much smaller amount of other materials with small molecules, such as the various salts and vitamins in food. This sort of diet, then, does not irritate such tender tissues as the mucous membrane of the upper part of the digestive tract.

Large amounts of sugar, however, especially if taken in concentrated form on an otherwise empty stomach, will be an irritant. You can actually see the irritation happening if you put a gastroscope into somebody's stomach, which allows you to see the stomach lining. If you now get him to swallow a moderately strong sugar solution—the equivalent, say, of four or five lumps in a cup of coffee—you can watch the mucous membrane turn red and angry as the irritant sugar reaches it.

The fact is that sugar in the quantities that are now part of the average Western diet, and especially in the way it is often taken on an empty stomach, will be a source of repeated irritation on the delicate mucous membranes of the oesophagus and the stomach. Irritation of the oesophagus is the most likely cause of heartburn. As for the stomach, it is not surprising that a high-sugar diet, even for only two weeks, can result in the production of more acid and much more active gastric juice, as we showed in our experiments. Finally, it is widely held that duodenal ulceration is a result of excessive secretion of gastric juice, so that it is also not difficult to see why sugar might contribute to the cause of this condition.

There is another possible way in which sugar might act on the stomach. As I have shown, sugar affects the adrenal gland, and it is known that some of the hormones produced by this gland increase the production of gastric juice. Sugar would then be producing its effects in the stomach both by a local action and by a general action.

Let me repeat that these suggestions are made simply because they constitute a reasonable explanation of at least some forms of severe indigestion. It remains to be seen whether these are the precise mechanisms by which sugar may contribute to the production of duodenal ulcer, for example. But even if the explanation turns out to be different, there is no doubt of the effectiveness in most patients of the low-carbohydrate diet in the relief of the symptoms of severe and chronic indigestion.

Surgeon-Captain T. L. Cleave, now retired from the British Navy, has suggested quite a different mechanism for the cause of peptic ulceration and other diseases of affluence. He believes that all "refined carbohydrate" is equally responsible. Both white flour and refined sugar cause peptic ulceration, he suggests, because they are concentrated—sugar being concentrated from cane or beet, and white flour from the whole wheat. He believes that it is the stripping of its protein that changes innocuous whole flour into ulcer-producing white flour. The idea behind this is that the protein is necessary for the proper neutralization of the gastric acid.

I do not find this theory convincing for three reasons. One is that the difference in the protein content between ordinary brown flour and white flour is very little, about 13.5 percent compared with 13.0 percent; the exact figures will depend on the sample of flour and the precise way it has been milled. But even flour made from whole wheat contains only a little more protein, perhaps 14.5 percent.

Secondly, bread is not the only source of protein, so that the neutralization of stomach acid does not depend entirely on bread, either brown or white. Bread contributes less than one-sixth of the average protein in Britain, where the total average daily intake is about one hundred grams a day. The difference between eating bread from the whole wheat and eating ordinary white bread is something like one gram of protein a day, and rather less if you eat the commoner sorts of brown bread rather than wholewheat bread.

Thirdly, our own experiments have shown that if the amount of starch in the diet, mostly from bread, is reduced and its place taken by sugar, there is a great change in gastric juice. The effects of bread and of sugar are too different for them to be lumped together as equally dangerous "refined carbohydrate."

GENERAL ACTION

While we don't know for certain how sugar can produce disease, I do believe that very dimly some sort of pattern is beginning to emerge. Now we must put up some reasonable theory based on this pattern, so that further experiments will reveal more of the pattern. Of course we shall have to change our theories if they turn out to be wildly (or even slightly) wrong.

In trying to understand how sugar can be involved in causing so many diseases and abnormalities, I have been especially impressed by two results of our work. One is that sugar produces an enlargement of the liver and kidneys of our experimental animals, not only by making all the cells swell up a little, but actually by increasing the number of cells in these organs. In technical terms, sugar produces not only hypertrophy but also hyperplasia.

The second effect that seems to be important is that sugar can produce, at least in some people, an increase in the level of insulin and a more striking increase in the level of adrenal cortical hormone; it also produces an enlargement of the adrenal glands in rats. It should be remembered, too, that these effects are more likely to occur when the blood is repeatedly flooded with high levels of the glucose and fructose produced when the sucrose is digested. This, in fact, is what happens, partly because—as the advertisement tells you—it is rapidly digested and absorbed, and partly because people so often take it in food and drink between meals when there is little else in the stomach to delay absorption.

To begin with, the effects on hormones and on liver and kidney should persuade any reasonable person that sugar is not just an ordinary kind of food. Secondly, its effect in producing an increase in hormone levels makes it possible to see how sugar can be implicated in such a large number of diseases. It also, I suggest, indicates why people may develop one disease rather than another disease. For the hormones maintain a most intricate interrelationship, both in the amounts circulating in the blood at any one time and in their actions on the body's metabolism. It seems to be always true that an increase in the amount of one hormone results in an increase or a decrease of several of the other hormones.

In a general way, the effect is a tendency to restore the state of the body to what it was before. This occurs because some of the actions of different hormones oppose one another, while some enhance one another. But the likelihood is that, after all the readjustments following the increase of one hormone, some actions of the whole group still are not in balance.

I would expect that the details of the ways in which these attempted readjustments are made vary from one person to another. Imagine a sudden flood of water into a stream. It eventually forces its way through a weak part of the bank. You now repair this rapidly, but you can fetch material only from some other parts of the bank—stones and gravel and mud and sand, a little from several places. When you have repaired the bridge, you have weakened other parts of the bank; only the next flood will tell you which part will now give away. It will depend on so many things, and two streams that seem to be identical will almost certainly behave differently when the stress comes.

Of course, you can pretend that the situation is really much simpler. It is not difficult to imagine that sugar causes diabetes because it makes the insulin-producing cells of the pancreas overwork until they become exhausted. And this may in fact be so for some sorts of diabetes. I say this because there is a growing belief that diabetes is not just one disease, or even the two diseases in the young and in the middle-aged to which I referred earlier. So there may be a complex mechanism by which sugar produces diabetes, or some sorts of diabetes, and not enough is known about the disease to try and unravel the mechanism.

With atherosclerosis, I have worked out the possible mechanism simply for my own benefit, because it gives us ideas of what new experiments we should undertake. This working hypothesis starts with the assumption that the underlying cause of the disease is a high level of insulin. The reasons for this belief are several.

First, most people who have definite atherosclerosis have a high level of insulin in the blood. Secondly, several circumstances increase the risk of coronary disease, and they include cigarette smoking, overweight, peripheral vascular disease, and maturity onset diabetes. Each of the first three, and often diabetes too, is associated with an increased level of insulin. Thirdly, reduction of overweight, or increased physical activity, both of which reduce the risk of developing coronary disease, result in a fall in insulin levels. Fourthly, experiments with rats have shown that administration of insulin produces an increased amount of cholesterol in the aorta. Finally, it does look as if some people are much more likely to get coronary thrombosis than other people are, so it would be understandable why only some people react to sugar by a raised level of insulin.

But the most cogent reason for believing that insulin, or perhaps some other hormone, underlies the process that ends as coronary disease is the multiplicity of changes that accompany the disease. As I have said several times, we are looking for the mechanism that produces a condition involving not only a raised level of cholesterol and triglycerides, but also a range of other disturbances: in biochemistry, in platelet behavior, and in a number of other characteristics. Only a disturbance of hormone levels is likely to afford an explanation of such a wide variety of disturbances.

At the moment it seems that the most likely first change is a rise in insulin level. But at least one other hormone is affected; as I showed, there is great interplay between the activities of the various hormones. It may therefore turn out that the first disturbance is in some hormone other than insulin, and that the rise in insulin level is secondary to this. We do not have nearly enough information yet to decide this question, but I am convinced that further work on hormonal activities is by now the most promising line of research that we should be pursuing.

In discussing the possible role of hormones in producing atherosclerosis, it is wise to remember that the sex hormones certainly play a part; that coronary disease is much more common in men than it is in women, but that the difference diminishes after the menopause when there is a diminution in the activity of the female sex hormones; and that there is a particularly close relationship between the hormones made by the sex glands and some of those made by the adrenal glands.

It is not yet possible to begin to describe how atherosclerosis develops; not enough is known about it. Yet it is perhaps worth some speculation. Let me suppose that the first change induced by a diet high in sucrose is a change in the amount of enzymes in body cells, such as the muscle cells. You can imagine that, over many years, a continuation of a high-sugar diet results in a decreased ability of the cells properly to carry out their normal metabolic processes. They now become unable properly to use their ordinary metabolic materials such as glucose, for which they require hormones, especially insulin. As a result, the level of glucose in the blood rises.

In order to overcome this disability in the cells, the pancreas increases the amount of insulin it makes and puts it into the blood stream. The increased insulin enables the cells now to deal with the glucose and other substances. At this point, the situation may lead to the condition of diabetes, or at least those manifestations of the disease called maturity onset diabetes. But insulin produces many other actions, and on many cells other than muscle cells, and these one may suppose were not affected by the sucrose in the diet. As far as these other activities are concerned there now exists an excessive amount of insulin. One result would be to change the balance of several of the other hormones. Another result would be to produce effects such as increased fat formation or obesity. And still other results would be to increase the accumulation of cholesterol and other fatty materials in the aorta, perhaps to change the properties of the platelets, and altogether gradually to produce the condition known as atherosclerosis.

Not all of these suggestions are original, although I have to take the responsibility of putting them all down here in what may ultimately turn out to be a quite nonsensical sequence. And I would be the first to agree that this is an extremely hypothetical picture.

I put it down, nevertheless, for two reasons: first, it indicates a possible role of sucrose in atherosclerosis that is not entirely implausible; secondly, it sets up an hypothesis that my colleagues and I can have in our minds to help us decide along what lines our further experiments should be directed.

I do not think it is worth pursuing my argument because so much has to be speculation. Let me only say that hormone changes certainly affect the skin, the rate of growth of an animal, and its sexual maturity, and that there is growing evidence of the relationship between hormones and some forms of cancer. Let me be content for now by saying that sugar produces many profound changes in body metabolism. It is therefore quite possible to imagine that it can be concerned in a wide range of diseases, including those such as diabetes and atherosclerosis which in themselves manifest profound disturbances of metabolism.

Microbes in the digestive tract

The third way in which sugar might act is by altering the numbers and proportions of the huge numbers of different microbes that inhabit the intestine. They exist and multiply on the residues of food that have not been absorbed or digested. The sorts of food that have been eaten will determine the kinds and amounts of these materials, which in turn will affect the proportion and numbers of the intestinal microbes.

Unfortunately, medical science is still not very knowledgeable about such details in human beings, although it is certain that changes are produced when sugar replaces starch in the diet.

While we do not yet know what effect these may have on the rest of the body, there does seem to be something to say about the replacement of part of the milk sugar (lactose) by ordinary sugar (sucrose) for babies. It is known that bottle-fed babies, who usually have sucrose added to increase the total sugar of cow's milk, tend to have gastroenteritis (diarrhea and vomiting) much more commonly than do breast-fed babies, who get only lactose. It has also been shown that the stools of breast-fed babies contain many more harmless lactobacilli than do the stools of bottle-fed babies, and far fewer of the potentially harmful coli bacteria. Again, stools of breast-fed babies tend to kill off added harmful bacteria; those from bottle-fed babies allow them to multiply.

These findings suggest that the contents of the intestine can make a baby either more or less susceptible to infection, and the research workers attribute this largely to the fact that bottle-fed babies get only part of the sugar as lactose and the rest as sucrose.

It has been suggested that diverticulitis, an uncomfortable disease of the large bowel associated with pain and diarrhea, may be in some way caused by modern diets. The most recent suggestion is that it comes from eating food with little residue, especially white bread instead of the more fibrous wholewheat bread. Earlier in this chapter I told you why I don't think one can explain duodenal ulcers and other diseases of Western man in this way. I do think that a possible cause of diverticulitis is the increase in sugar intake at the expense of starch. The different types and numbers of microbes that occur when this dietary change is made could well influence the bowel itself, altering both its activity and its resistance to damage.

Sucrose in the blood

I pointed out that all sugar that is eaten is digested into glucose and fructose before it is absorbed into the blood. This digestion is usually quite complete except when very large amounts of sugar are consumed; in that event very small amounts of undigested sucrose can get into the blood stream. As we are beginning to find out, sucrose has several potent actions in living cells, and so it is quite conceivable that these tiny amounts can, over a long period of time, produce damaging effects on the body tissues. This is at present pure hypothesis, but it is a suggestion that future research must pursue.

16

Why Sugar Should Be Banned

One of the very satisfactory features of my department of nutrition has been the generally friendly relationship we have had with the food industry. This is true even though, in giving people advice about what to eat, we also tell them what *not* to eat. Since few people in the affluent countries are eating too little and many are eating too much, telling people to eat more of some foods necessarily results in telling them to eat less of other foods. We were thus often giving advice that was directly against the interests of one or other of the food organizations. Still, most of the firms with which we were in contact managed to maintain a friendly relationship with us, even though they sometimes told us quite forthrightly what they thought of our activities.

And when I say "friendly relationships," I mean much more than an occasional invitation to lunch. Since we began building up the nutrition department in newly built laboratories in 1960, I calculate that we have had grants from the food industry amounting to the best

part of half a million pounds—well over one million
dollars.

It is clear that a great deal of our recent research,
as this book shows, has been concerned with the possible harmful effects of a high consumption of sugar,
so that we have increasingly caused unease among many
of our industrial friends. Since such a very large proportion of manufactured foods contains sugar, and many
of them a great deal, it was to be expected that our
relations with one or two friends in industry have
occasionally become rather strained.

There have, in fact, been many different reactions,
and they were well summarized when I had occasion
to meet the four or five directors of a large food-
manufacturing firm whose wide range of products includes a considerable quantity of chocolate and sugar
candies. This was several years ago, when the case
against sugar was not so strong as it is today, but I
nevertheless put this question to them:

Supposing our opinion turns out to be backed by
incontrovertible evidence that sugar, and consequently
some of your products, contribute significantly to deaths
due to coronary disease; would you then continue to
make your luscious, mouth-watering chocolates?

The range of replies represents the whole range of
attitudes I have found among others with whom I
have discussed the question of what to do about the
high consumption of sugar, which now, without doubt,
contributes to so much disease and death. At one extreme there was the director who said it was not his
job to protect people from themselves; he was not
forcing people to eat his products, and if they chose
to do so at the risk of harming themselves, it was of
their own free choice. At the other extreme, a director
said that, if he were convinced that sugar was dangerous

to health, he would resign from the company; in the same way, he said, nothing would induce him now to be a director of, or even own shares in, a company that made cigarettes.

Several other views fell between these two extremes. One came from a director who said that, if the evidence against sugar became strong, he would encourage his firm to spend money and effort into research designed to find ways of combating its ill-effects—some sort of antidote, for example, that they might put into their products. At this writing, they are still only looking into the possible use of sugar alternatives.

My own view? This is based on the belief that I expressed earlier—that people have become increasingly able to separate wants and needs, to an extent that the satisfaction of wants without hindrance can be disastrous for the individual and for the human species. Man always wanted to eat sweet foods because he liked them. So long as the only sweet foods he could find were fruit, by satisfying his wants for sweetness he helped to satisfy his needs for vitamin C and other nutrients. But since he began to produce his own foods, and especially since he developed the technology of sugar refining and food manufacture, he has been able to produce and separate sweetness from all nutrients. What he wants is no longer necessarily what he needs. Because of the strong drives that originally served important biological purposes, it is not enough to say that people should be told what is good for them, and what is bad, and then left to make their own decisions.

In fact, this alleged principle of knowledge coupled with free choice is not so inviolable as is sometimes made out. It is accepted in most countries that people should not have a free choice to smoke opium, if they wish, or to sniff cocaine. So the only question is: at

what point should the community intervene to protect
individuals from following those instincts that our
technological skill has made it dangerous to follow?

A continuum stretches from a situation where society
should obviously interfere—the smoking of opium, say
—to a situation where we should not—indeed, cannot
effectively interfere short of erecting a police state—for
example, the taking of insufficient exercise. Somewhere
in between these two extremes lies the smoking of
cigarettes and the consumption of sugar.

I am one of those who believe that the community
should be taking stronger steps to discourage cigarette
smoking: perhaps short of declaring it illegal but certainly beyond such almost completely ineffective steps
as banning advertising on television or putting warning
notices on the packages. The very least that should
be done would be to institute an intensive program of
research into methods of effective persuasion on how
to give up smoking, or how not to begin it.

Sadly, there has been insufficient official appreciation
of the need to study seriously the efficacy of the various
techniques of persuasion, in the same way as one
might study the efficacy of the various techniques of
surgery in the cure of disease. This indifference was
explicitly brought out a few years ago when a member
of Parliament asked whether the British Medical Research Council was looking into ways in which people
might be influenced to give up smoking. The answer
from the government minister concerned was that this
was not the proper job of the Medical Research Council. One fears that the same reply would be given today
to the question of how to persuade people to stop
taking sugar.

One reason why people are reluctant to believe that
it is necessary to do anything about studying the art

of persuasion is that they do not appreciate the wide gap that exists between knowledge and behavior— between knowing and doing. It is commonly believed that all you have to do in the way of health education is to inform people. Just tell them that eating sweets makes holes in their teeth, and your job is done. And it is only slowly being realized, even by such United Nations special agencies as the World Health Organization and the Food and Agriculture Organization, that this approach is one of the main causes of the failure of health education in developing countries. It simply is not good enough just to tell people that they should eat eggs, or give their babies milk; there is a lot more to it than that.

Let me pursue this a moment longer. And again let me take cigarette smoking as an example. Persuasion to give up cigarette smoking usually proceeds in several stages. When you are told that you should give it up because it causes lung cancer, you may well begin by saying, as so many smokers once did, that you don't believe it. So the first step is to persuade you that it is true. If this is successful, you will say, "Yes, I now believe that smoking causes lung cancer, but I don't think it's likely to hit me, so I don't think it's worthwhile giving it up." The next stage of a persuasion effort will be reached only when you say, "I know smoking causes lung cancer, and I really should give it up, but I just can't, even though I've tried." The next step comes when you are able to say, "I know that smoking is harmful, and I have stopped smoking." And the final step is when you can say, "I haven't smoked for years, and I don't believe I'd ever start up again."

Clearly, nothing short of this last could be counted as effective health education. It is not effective if you stop at the stage of changing attitudes; the test for effectiveness must be a permanent change of behavior.

I have seen many campaigns backed by dental authorities to reduce dental decay in school children. Sometimes they are content simply when they have produced attractive posters; sometimes they go further and give prizes to children who can answer questions about the structure of teeth and how the process of tooth decay occurs. But rarely have they tested whether their propaganda has in fact resulted in a reduction in the number of decayed teeth, even though nothing short of this is really of any use.

We once carried out a survey among London housewives to see how much they know about nutrition, and what they did about it. Here are two examples of what we found. Nine out of ten housewives said that brown bread is nutritionally superior to white bread (which incidentally, as I showed, is not true); yet in spite of this firm belief, 92 percent of bread sold in Britain is white bread. Again, nine out of ten housewives were sure that their children got tooth decay from eating sweets. Yet the British are easily the world's largest consumers of candy, not to speak of the additional sugar children get in cakes, cookies, ice cream, and other foods and drinks. Yet it is rare to find much effort by the children's mothers to control this consumption, and these are the same mothers who know what this does to the teeth.

Considering examples such as these, you can understand why I believe that it is just not good enough to assume that the danger of eating sugar will be dealt with satisfactorily just by making sure that people are informed; that people will stop taking these foods and drinks once they know that sugar is involved in causing not only overweight and dental decay, but also heart disease, chronic indigestion, ulcers, and diabetes, and perhaps a number of other diseases. The likely outcome is, as it has been with cigarette smoking, that some people will be persuaded to stop, but the very large majority will do nothing about it, even if one can convince them of the harm that sugar does.

Should society then in some way coerce people to give up sugar? Most people would answer this question with a very firm "No." It is enough, they believe, that people should be informed about the value of different foods, good or bad, and then left to make their own choice. I have given my own reasons for thinking that our ability to separate palatability from nutritional value makes this an unrealistic view. Moreover, the idea that free choice is sufficient implies that the choice is in fact free; that people do have total and unbiased access to knowledge about food values. But do they?

Those who, like myself, are worried about excessive consumption of sugar—dentists, for example—often point to the enormous volume of advertising for candy, cakes, ice cream, soft drinks. In Britain alone, something like twenty-five million dollars a year is spent in advertising these goods, which amounts to 10 percent of the value of their total retail sales. But I am not sure that advertising does very much to increase the total amount consumed. There is some evidence that the effect of advertising is, rather, to persuade people to buy one brand instead of another brand—Coca-Cola instead of Pepsi-Cola.

There are more subtle ways in which advertising, public relations, and other methods of marketing act to sustain a high consumption of particular products. I once prepared a reducing diet for an organization that obviously wanted to publicize its own particular foods. I did this without the slightest twinge of conscience because it happens that I have always recommended these foods as being highly nutritious and highly desirable in any sensible diet, reducing or otherwise. At the same time as I recommended these foods in a reducing diet, I naturally mentioned other foods that should be restricted, and it will not surprise you to hear that sugar ranked pretty high in this list. But it *may* surprise you that as soon as the diet began to be distributed I was pressed to withdraw the reference to the curtailment of sugar consumption, and you will have guessed that this request came from a sugar company. You will also have guessed that I did not comply.

The most subtle way for advertising to affect the sale of a product is through one rule of most advertising media: they will not accept copy that attacks other products—"knocking copy." Basically, it is a sound principle; you should try and sell your products—your beer, or brassières, or bookcases—on their own merits, pointing out what is good about them rather than what is bad about your competitors' products. But you can see the difficulties encountered if you produce a new drink sweetened without sugar, or a new baby food with milk sugar (lactose) instead of ordinary sugar.

Your whole objective is to persuade people to take your food on the basis that ordinary sugar is harmful. Once again, I am thinking of a specific situation where the manufacturer of a baby food was dissuaded from making this point in its advertising. I am not convinced that the media control their advertising entirely for the benefit of the consumer; I feel they tend to look over their shoulders just a little nervously to make sure that they have not offended the advertisers or their agents.

And I am frankly very skeptical when I read the claims of the British and American advertising industry that they always have the interests of the community at heart. Recently the chairman of the British Advertising Association said that its objectives included "Keeping the pathway open for honest advertising—paving it with honesty, widening it with new understanding, getting it recognized as a utility serving the community as a whole." I am sure every one can think of examples of advertising that fall far short of keeping these objectives.

If one keeps in mind examples of how information can be distorted or withheld (and these examples are only a few that have come the way of only one person), it becomes even more evident why people should not be left entirely to themselves to decide what they should or should not eat. Sooner or later, I feel, it will be necessary to introduce legislation that by some means or other will prevent people from consuming so much sugar, and especially prevent parents, relatives, and friends from ruining the health of babies and children.

But so long as this is not considered a public health matter, is there nothing we ourselves can do?

First, not all people will have the same problem. Some people find it quite easy to give up sugar, but many find it really difficult. Let me tell you how I managed.

I must now confess that I used to be about the most dedicated sugar "addict" you have ever seen. I stress this for two reasons. One reason is that a lot of people imagine that my campaign against sugar comes about just because I don't like sweet things; if only they knew how many pounds of milk chocolate and candy and cakes of all sorts I used to tuck away each week! At a rough guess, I would say that my total sugar consumption must have been not less than ten ounces a day, probably nearer fifteen. The second reason for this confession is to show that it is possible to break the sugar habit. I have cut down from five or six pounds a week to at most two or three ounces a week—sometimes next to nothing—and if I can do it, so can you.

The first thing, of course, is to have the incentive. You must make up your mind quite firmly that you really want to cut down your sugar intake. It may be that you are beginning to worry about your waistline or your dentist's bills, even if you don't really believe all I have said about ulcers and diabetes and heart disease. Once you have made up your mind, then you won't find it too difficult. But start slowly.

If you take two spoons or lumps of sugar in your coffee or tea, cut the amount down to one for a week or two, and only then stop altogether. Try not to drink the usual soft drinks. Drink low-calorie drinks instead or iced tea; and what is wrong with plain water? If you really cannot cut down on your beer or wine, choose the dry varieties. And avoid the sweet "mixers" for your whiskey or gin or vodka.

You can also cut down gradually on puddings and ice cream, and you can look out for the less sweet varieties of cakes and cookies. Keep off the sugar-coated cereals for breakfast, and don't sprinkle sugar on them!

You may find it difficult to believe, but when you have really become used to taking very little sugar in your foods and drinks, you will notice that all your foods have a wide range of interesting flavors that you had forgotten. Swamping everything with sugar tends to hide these flavors and blunts the sensitivity of your palate. You will especially notice how much you enjoy fruit—all the subtle differences between one sort of apple or pear or orange and another. And unless you eat a couple of pounds or more of fresh fruit a day, you can't possibly get to eat as much as the average person now eats of refined sugar, let alone the amount that so many people eat.

All this does *not* mean that you must never, in any circumstances, take a piece of pie or a helping of ice cream. No great harm will come to you if, at a dinner party, you accept something special that your hostess has made for the occasion. Eating sensibly is not the same as making a nuisance of yourself.

There are clearly some sources of sugar that are likely to give you much more than do other sources. If you find that you usually put two or three pieces of sugar in your tea and coffee, and if you add up and find you are taking seven or eight cups a day, you can easily see that this is a chance of reducing your sugar by two or three ounces a day. Add the amount you take with your breakfast cereal, and perhaps in the occasional cola or fruit drink during the day, and you will find that it is not a great hardship to get down to a quarter of your usual intake or even much less.

It is more than likely that the harmful effects of sugar are greater when you consume it with little else. In this way, its digestion and absorption are not hampered by the digestion and absorption of other foods, so that the blood stream is quickly flooded with sugar. So it is more important to avoid sugar taken between meals, for example in drinks and candy, than to take, say, a piece of apple pie at the end of the meal. The digestion and absorption of the sugar will now be very much slower and its effects much less.

Perhaps the most difficult problem is how to bring up your children without smothering them with sugar. Everything in the modern way of living seems to conspire to thrust sugar down their innocent and uncomplaining throats, almost from the moment they are born. But with a little care you can at least see that your child does not get into the "two-or-three-pounds-of-sugar-a-week" bracket.

You should begin by choosing one of the baby formulas that is made up with added milk sugar (lactose) instead of ordinary sugar. Next, when you introduce cereals or more extensive mixed feeding, choose instant or canned foods that definitely do not mention sugar on the label, or take the trouble to make your own strained meats and vegetables. Make sure the orange juice has had no sugar added to it or make up your own.

Later, by all means give a child an occasional candy or cookie, but really only occasionally and as a treat. Never, of course, give it at bedtime after your child has cleaned his teeth. A good plan is to get your little one to clean his teeth after every occasion when he has eaten a candy or cookie. Ask him when he comes home from school or from a visit to grandma if he has had a candy; if so, get him to clean his teeth straight away. With luck, he may get bored with so much teeth cleaning and be content with sweet foods only at mealtimes. And after meals you will no doubt want him to brush his teeth in any case.

In the end, the real difficulty is not so much how you bring up your child but how much kind friends and relatives, often behind your back, press candy into his little hand. Although you may not be able to keep him away from sugar as much as you wish, you will find it quite possible to keep the amount of sugar down to far less than so many children now have.

You will have noticed, by the way, that I prefer the low-calorie soft drinks to those that contain sugar. You will see from this that I do not at all accept that you run any risk from taking the saccharine that they contain. Nor would I mind if you took cyclamate, except that for reasons that I think are quite irrelevant, cyclamate has now been banned in many countries. My own view is that it is highly unlikely that cyclamate does anybody any harm, while there is no doubt whatever that sugar can do a very great deal of harm.

You may decide that it is better to wean yourself entirely from taking sweet foods and drinks, and that you can do this more readily by avoiding the use of sugar substitutes altogether. This is a decision you must make yourself; all that matters is that you should take as little sugar as you can.

Before you begin to reduce your sugar intake, and again at the end of your first week, make a list of all the sugar you have consumed on an average day. Make a rough calculation on the basis of this table, and see how much you have saved since you began. In particular, see whether you have reduced your intake to less than fifty grams a day (nearly two ounces) in your first week; then see how long it takes you to get down to twenty grams a day.

Sugar content of some foods and drinks

1 piece of sugar	4	grams
1 flat teaspoon of sugar	5	"
1 bottle of cola	12	"
1 glass of "fruit drink"	20	"
1 spoon jelly, jam, or marmalade	5	"
1 2-oz. piece of cake	10	"
1 4-oz. piece of apple pie	20	"
1 2-oz. piece of chocolate	30	"
1 oz. candy	20	"
1 2-oz. ice cream	12	"

17

The Sugar Industry's
Defense Strategy: Attack

One way in which the sugar industry responds to attack is to try and put pressure on other food industries that seem to be drawing attention to the harmful effects of sugar.

I once gave a talk that was sponsored by one of the large international food manufacturers. It was published in a book, together with several other talks on nutrition by other research workers. In my talk, I had occasion to refer to research on the undesirable qualities of sugar. Soon after the book was produced, the chairman of the food company that had organized the talks and was distributing the book was approached by the chairman of a sugar refining company and asked to stop the distribution of the book because it would not be seemly for one food manufacturer to "knock" the product of another. After some argument the book's distributor agreed to do this; what the sugar man did not know was that only two out of the several thousand printed copies had not yet been sent out.

An obvious way to respond to attack is simply to deny its basis; an even more subtle way is to claim that exactly the opposite is true. If most people say that sugar causes dental decay, you keep on publishing advertisements or short articles that stress how sugar is not important; what is important is constitutional proneness to dental decay or whether one uses the toothbrush often enough. When most people say that sugar makes people fat, you mount a campaign claiming that, in fact, sugar makes you slim. I cited some such examples earlier.

The most intensive publicity activity of the sugar industry during the past ten or twelve years has been its attack on cyclamate. This campaign was pursued even though, as I showed, sugar interests like to claim immunity from attack by other food producers.

First, the sugar industry spent a great deal of money on actual research on the possible harmful effects of cyclamate; very much more money, incidentally, than they have ever spent on studying the metabolic effects of their own product. They announced the scope of this research repeatedly in their information reports right up to 1969, when cyclamate was banned.

Their activities began quite early. In 1953, they began to spend at the rate of $600,000 a year, and increased this to $750,000 in 1957. And here is what an American advertising agency said in 1954 to defend the sugar industry's spending so much money on publicity:

"These substitutes might never command a really damaging share of market in terms of bottles, cans, and cases, but their share of market in terms of human prejudice might be very damaging indeed. This obviously calls for a broad program of information about sugar among consumers. It is the only real insurance the industry can have."

By 1964 the sugar industry had come to the conclusion that artificial sweeteners really were a serious challenge. The president of Sugar Information, Incorporated, talking to the Sugar Club, then said: "Every man in this room is affected directly, in the pocketbook, by the challenge of the synthetic sweeteners. I want to discuss with you the nature of this challenge, its dimensions and its impact. I want to tell you what we are doing to meet it." He then went on to describe an advertising campaign "questioning the value of synthetic sweetened soft drinks."

From that time, the industry directly and blatantly attacked cyclamate. Here is a part of one advertisement:

"Sugar's got what it takes. It's instant energy. Soft drinks made with sugar give you something to go on. But 'syntha-colas' made with chemicals only give you a wet, sweet taste."

Some of the experiments with cyclamate that the sugar people sponsored were really very badly carried out. For example, in one experiment rats were fed with a diet containing 5% of cyclamate, which is equivalent in sweetening power to sugar amounting to 150% of the diet! Nobody should therefore be surprised that the rats did not thrive on this diet, and that they did not grow as well as did rats without cyclamate. Even if the cyclamate were only 2% of the diet, it would be equivalent to a person eating 13 ounces of sugar a day, and I have already shown what that amount does to people and animals.

The great scientific discovery of what a 5% cyclamate diet does to the growth of rats was very widely publicized, not only in articles in many magazines, but in an information brochure sent to every member of Parliament in Britain.

The chief irony of the cyclamate story is that the eventual banning of this sweetener in the United States was the result of research sponsored by Abbott Laboratories, which was the world's largest manufacturer of cyclamate. In this research, carried out by the Food and Drug Research Laboratories in Maspeth, New York, rats were given enormous doses of cyclamate along with saccharine—the equivalent of 11 pounds of sugar a day for an adult. At the end of two years (a very long time in the life of a rat) a few animals showed the beginnings of cancer of the bladder.

Ordinarily, one would now get a group of experts together to try and evaluate the relevance of these studies to the consumption of something like one-fiftieth of the equivalent dose in man, which would be about the average person's cyclamate consumption. The decision, however, was predetermined by the so-called Delaney Clause in the American food and drug laws. This says that a material that, in any dose, causes cancer in any animal must not be used in human food.

So cyclamate was banned in America and then in several other countries, thereby presumably inviting everybody to go on eating all the sugar they want.

There is also a personal twist to these experiments and results. When I have reported some of the experiments that my colleagues and I have done, with perhaps as much as fifteen ounces of sugar a day in young men but often a lot less, I am told that these are abnormally high amounts and that our results therefore are not valid. In fact, these quantities are not unheard of in quite ordinary people, as I showed in Chapter 5. In any case, they are nowhere near the equivalent of the astronomical amounts of cyclamate that had to be used in order to show how "dangerous" this material is.

I said that the sugar industry has supported very little research about what sugar does in the body, although it did, it is true, support some research on sugar and dental caries. I myself have several times invited the International Sugar Research Foundation to support the work we are doing in my laboratory, on the grounds that the sugar people themselves ought to be the first to know whether their product does, in fact, produce ill effects. Two or three times it really appeared that they were going to help us financially in our research, but each time the suggestion fell through.

Recently, the International Sugar Research Foundation was begun to support some work on the possible relationship between sugar and atherosclerosis. A research report appeared in the middle of 1971 from Wake Forest University in North Carolina. A dozen miniature pigs were fed on diets with sugar and compared with a dozen that were fed without sugar. Six pigs in each group were killed at the end of one year; the remaining six in each group were killed at the end of two years.

The International Sugar Research Foundation has triumphantly claimed that the results prove that sugar does nothing either to the cholesterol level or to the development of atherosclerosis. A careful look at the results, however, shows that the cholesterol in the sugar group was, as it happened, somewhat lower than that of the control group at the beginning of the experiment; thereafter it was almost continuously higher. Moreover, more atherosclerosis was, in fact, found in the sugar-fed pigs than in the control pigs.

Is it any wonder that one sometimes becomes quite despondent about whether it is worthwhile to try to do scientific research in matters of health? The results may be of great importance in helping people to avoid disease, but you then find that they are being misled by propaganda designed to promote commercial interests in a way that you thought only existed in bad B films.

18

The Honest Manufacturer and the Objective Scientist

When I began to write this book, I had no intention of writing this chapter. People usually don't like hearing other people's grumbles, especially when they feel they can't themselves do very much about them. And it is also rather embarrassing to complain in public—rather like a wife's telling you about her husband's peccadillos, or a friend's telling you he is being subtly pestered by his landlord. You would rather not hear about it; if you have to hear about it, you find yourself thinking that it is probably at least partly the wife's fault, or your friend's fault—anything that will relieve your feelings of guilt, because you really can't think of what to do without getting much more involved than you would like.

But I am perhaps misleading you. This chapter is not really written to provoke your sympathy but just to tell you, coolly and quietly, some of the things that can happen to a scientist who makes discoveries and holds opinions that a lot of people don't like, and who nevertheless feels that, since they can affect the health of millions of people, these facts and opinions should be told to the people whenever an occasion arises.

First, let me tell you about the reaction I have had from "ordinary" people, by which I mean people who are not doctors or scientists. And ordinary people, by the way, have a very curious idea of what a nutritionist is or does.

I once gave a lunchtime lecture to a lay audience of women—a very crowded audience, I am conceited enough to say—for some charitable cause. My hostess and her committee had gone to a lot of trouble to make sure that the lunch would be to my liking—nut cutlets, green salad with grated carrot, fresh live yoghurt brought from a special place some twenty miles away. As some of my readers will know, this is not the sort of diet I normally eat, or especially recommend. There is nothing wrong with it, if you like that sort of food, nor is there anything wrong with a slice of beef or a steak, or a couple of boiled eggs, and there is nothing wrong either with a glass of milk instead of the yoghurt bought at great expense and inconvenience.

I tell you this just to illustrate the point that many people imagine that a nutritionist is just a special sort of food crank, and that most of the time he is telling you to eat rather odd food. Whenever I am dining out at some public function, I see people at adjoining tables craning in their chairs to see what is on my plate.

More than this, whenever he gets a chance, the nutritionist is supposed to react like Johnny's mother, who says to his older sister, "Find out what Johnny's doing and tell him not to." In the same way, lots of people have the idea that I spend my time finding out what they like to eat, and then telling them not to.

This notion of how a nutritionist supposedly thinks

and behaves largely explains, I believe, the reaction of many ordinary people to what I have been saying and writing in the last few years about sugar. First, they know that lots of people who are slightly cranky about their food don't eat refined sugar, only brown sugar, and so they have the idea that I, too, am saying the same sort of thing. By now you will have realized that sugar is sugar is sugar.

Secondly, since they have the idea that I belong to the band that says that everything you enjoy is illegal, immoral, or fattening, they think it is quite understandable that I should tell them to avoid all those lovely sugary things like cakes and ice cream and chocolate. One of my American critics has actually called me "the English nutritionist who seems to be committed to the doctrine that sugar is the source of all evil other than that attributable to original sin."

All in all, these reactions have resulted in a not very serious response to my attempts to persuade the public to reduce their consumption of sugar.

Holes in the teeth?

Well, they all know about that, but they have never really believed that dental decay is a very serious condition.

Heart disease, diabetes, and so on?

Well, they have heard so much talk about these conditions, and everyone seems to have different ideas about what causes them—and anyway we have got to die sometime, so why make life miserable by giving up all those delicious sugary foods and drinks?

It may be that there are some people, perhaps even many people, who have taken sufficient notice of what I have been saying to reduce their sugar intake. Certainly I do meet people in Britain from time to time who tell me with enthusiasm how they have done so and how much better they feel; and this is in addition to those few patients we have treated in our research and whom nothing on earth would persuade to go back to their previous ways of eating. But I still don't believe we have influenced more than a very small proportion of the people who have heard or read of our work.

I have already said how much help I and my department have had from the food industry, and how much I appreciate that this help was often given by food manufacturers whose products were at the same time being strenuously condemned by me. But it would have been unrealistic for me to imagine that support for our work was universally forthcoming from every one of the firms we approached.

One interesting incident arose when we were seeking funds for an extension of the nutrition department, and an appeal was made to most of the large food companies. We had a most generous response, though not all, of course, felt able to subscribe. But one firm thought it necessary to explain the reasons why it was not going to contribute to our appeal. Professor Yudkin, the letter said, has once again been reported in the daily press as saying that he thought sugar was harmful. Well, it was bad enough for him to *hold* such views, and even worse for him to publicize them in this way. Worst of all, he actually taught these views to his students! (I am not at all sure what a university teacher is supposed to teach, if he is not to teach what he believes.)

A more interesting incident occurred in 1964. In the spring of that year, I received an invitation from a recently formed French organization, FIPAL—La Fondation pour le Progrès de l'Alimentation. It introduced itself as an organization supported by the French food industry, whose object was to promote the study of food and nutrition and the dissemination of knowledge about these subjects. Its purposes, the letter continued, were entirely scientific and had nothing at all to do with the commercial objectives of the supporting industrial firms.

FIPAL was going to hold its first scientific conference in Paris in November, 1964, when it intended to discuss the subject of man's food habits. Since they knew of my interest and research work in this field, would I please accept this invitation to take part in the conference and read a paper about our work and our views on this subject?

The few inquiries I was able to make, and a list of the other scientists that were going to take part, persuaded me that this was a body with truly scientific aims. So I wrote that I happily agreed to participate, and we began some correspondence about the details.

A few months later, I received a letter from the secretary saying he was worried about articles appearing in the French press reporting some of my work that had just been published in the British medical journal *Lancet,* in which I was supposed to have produced evidence that the consumption of sugar might be involved in causing heart disease. The secretary of FIPAL said that he was now writing in his other capacity, as the person in charge of public relations for the French sugar refining industry. He assumed that the newspapers had misunderstood or at least grossly exaggerated the work I had published; you know, he said, what newspapers are like.

I assured him that the newspaper accounts were pretty accurate, as he would see from the original *Lancet* article that I was now sending him; that I had not realized that this might embarrass him or indeed embarrass FIPAL; and that under the circumstances it would be a good idea if I were to withdraw from the forthcoming meeting. By return mail I received an agitated reply. Of course there was no question of my withdrawing from the FIPAL meeting; his previous letter had simply been one of inquiry to know if the newspaper accounts were accurate; that was all he wanted to know. He assured me once again that FIPAL's aims were to obtain and disseminate scientific information without any bias whatever.

So I went to Paris in the autumn. The contributors, including myself, read their papers on a Friday, and I then spent most of the weekend closeted with two or three members of the secretariat in preparing summaries of the contributions and arranging the details of the following Monday's discussion meetings.

A year or more after these events, I received another letter from the secretary. He was finalizing the papers presented at the meeting for publication as a book. He referred to my paper in which I had spoken of the importance of palatability in determining what people ate; I had specially spoken of the high palatability of sugar's being responsible for its high consumption, and had said that I believed there was growing evidence that sugar could play a part in some of the diseases of affluence such as heart disease.

Would I mind, asked FIPAL's secretary, if he omitted the offending passage—it was only one or two sentences—or, alternatively, could he put in an asterisk at this point, referring to a footnote in which I would say that this was only my own personal view and in fact most other people did not agree with it?

In my reply, I said I could not reconcile this request with his original and repeated assurance that FIPAL was a scientific organization that was not intended to concern itself with commercial interests. I did not agree, therefore, to having my article censored. Moreover, like any other author, I took it for granted that what I wrote would be understood as giving my own personal view and no one else's, so that it would be ludicrous to write the sort of footnote he requested. There was a third possibility, and that was that he might wish to omit my article altogether.

And this is what happened. The published report of the conference gives my name as a participant, but you will not find in it the paper I read.

So far I have spoken of the reaction of the public and the food manufacturers to our work on the possible role of sugar in producing disease, especially heart disease. What about my fellow scientists? Here at least, you will probably say, I have been able to obtain a careful, unemotional, logical assessment of the evidence that we and others have produced.

But one of the things that has taken me a long time to learn is that scientists as a group are no more, and no less, influenced by emotional and irrational reactions than other people are. Certainly, many of my scientific colleagues, in many countries around the world, have followed our work and that of other research workers and have become pretty convinced that there is a good case for believing that the high current consumption of sugar by so many people is a cause of a variety of diseases, including coronary disease. Some others are not convinced, but are reasonably impressed with the evidence that is accumulating and are prepared to be convinced when more evidence is forthcoming. Some are entirely unconvinced, and give the impression that nothing will make them believe the story.

I have often wondered what determines this sort of opinion. I suppose one reason must be the same as that which I noted before: most people like sweet foods and drinks, and resent being told that what they like is bad for them. Then there are those scientists who have accepted the view that coronary thrombosis is due largely to a high consumption of fat, and are—perhaps unconsciously—reluctant to admit that they were wrong. Basically, a similar group are those who have all along *not* accepted the view that fat is a cause of heart disease and have denied that diet plays any part, extending this negative view to sugar.

These paragraphs will, I know, not endear me to my colleagues. Even many who are my friends will believe that I should not be writing like this; some are themselves so reasonable and gentle and—dare I say it?—so naïve that they will believe I have no justification for casting aspersions on the reasonableness of fellow scientists. The two following examples will perhaps serve to disillusion them about the supposedly inevitable and irreproachable rationality of scientists.

It was suggested by some of my Swiss acquaintances that I come to Switzerland and tell them about our recent research results, especially as they related to coronary disease. They put it to a leading physician that I be invited to talk to the important medical society of which he was at the time the president. His reply was that he knew all about our work on coronary disease, that it was based entirely on the epidemiological finding that there is a lot of coronary disease in populations that eat a lot of sugar, and that this did not impress him at all, since these populations also had several other characteristics in diet as well as in other respects.

So here was a scientist, clearly quite unaware of all the research that we and others had published over the past six or eight years, and yet claiming to be knowledgeable in the subject and in consequence feeling quite justified in dismissing an opportunity to hear more about our work.

I have already mentioned Dr. Ancel Keys and his pioneer work in relation to diet and heart disease. A year or so ago he wrote a memorandum, which he sent to a large number of scientists working in this field, and which, with very few changes, has now been published in a medical journal, *Atherosclerosis*. It consists entirely of a strong criticism—I nearly said virulent criticism—of the work I have published from time to time on the theory that sugar is the main dietary factor involved in causing heart disease.

The publication contains a number of quite incorrect and unjustified statements; for instance: that we had never tested our method for measuring sugar intake; that no one eats the amounts of sugar that we and others have used in our experiments; that it was absurd of me in 1957 to use international statistics of forty-one countries as evidence for the relationship between sugar and heart disease (exactly the same statistics that Dr. Keys had previously used for only six selected countries to show the relationship between fat and heart disease).

He ends by triumphantly pointing out that both sugar and fat intakes are related to heart disease, but that the cause must be fat, not sugar, because he had just found in 1970 that fat intake and sugar intake are themselves closely linked. You will remember my own discussion of this link in Chapter 5, based on the fact that as far back as 1964 I had shown this relationship to exist between fat intake and sugar intake. Let me therefore quote from a recently published book, *Pathogenesis of Coronary Artery Disease*, written by Dr. Meyer Friedman, another distinguished worker in this field:

It is sad, for example, to observe that essentially honorable investigators omit published data (including some of their own data obtained earlier) which refute or call into question their contemporary data and the interpretations they made of them. It is even sadder to observe how these same observers eagerly and indiscriminately collect studies (no matter how poorly or incompletely performed) supporting their respective hypotheses, but peruse with the most "nit-picking" and distrustful eye other studies which tend to subvert the interpretive verity of their own. But this is not really a very important cause of our present confusion because only a few investigators indulge in these practices, and their foibles are quite well known to their scientific peers. They essentially succeed in misleading only themselves and those physicians and laymen who can not be expected to know of the self-imposed enslavement of the investigators to their respective concepts.

One final point. There is, I am afraid, still a common feeling among academics of all callings that it is not quite nice for a university professor to appear on the radio or television or in the popular press and talk to ordinary people about his work. According to this view, the academic should remain in the quiet cloisters of his university, concern himself with high thinking that may have little to do with everyday life, and discuss his work only with his fellow academics. If he does not do this, then the value and importance of his own research work is inevitably diminished in the eyes of many in the academic establishment.

I have already stated my own point of view on this matter. I do not think it is justified for a research worker, scientist or non-scientist, to refuse to communicate any part of his speciality to the non-specialist who may be or could become interested. Least of all do

I believe it is justified for anyone concerned with matters of health to refuse to discuss his own work or his own ideas with anyone in the community when he has reason to believe that he can help them toward better health, and when he is quite certain that his advice cannot possibly impair their health.

For, in spite of all the reasons that, as I have shown, stand in the way of people following this advice, I nevertheless know that some are influenced. This is as great a satisfaction to me as the removal of a virulently infected appendix must be a cause of satisfaction to a surgeon. And, although I know it sounds pretentious, as a subscriber to the Hippocratic oath, I am sure that it is just as important to help people to avoid disease as it is to help to cure disease.

Selected Bibliography

R. Ardrey, *African Genesis*, Atheneum, New York, 1961

W. R. Aykroyd, *The Story of Sugar*, Quadrangle, Chicago, 1967

M. O. Bruker, *Zucker und Gesundheit*, Verlag Schwabe, Bad Homburg, 1965

E. Cheraskin, W. M. Ringsdorf and J. W. Clark, *Diet and Disease*, Rodale, Pennsylvania, 1968

T. L. Cleave, G. D. Campbell and N. S. Painter, *Diabetes, Coronary Thrombosis and the Saccharine Disease* (2nd edition), John Wright, Bristol, 1969

R. Dart, *Beyond Antiquity*, South African Broadcasting Co.

Noel Deer, *The history of sugar*, Chapman & Hall, London, 1949

Goeffrey Fairrie, *Sugar*, Fairrie and Company Ltd., Liverpool, 1925

Meyer Friedman, *Pathogenesis of Coronary Artery Disease*, McGraw-Hill, New York, 1969

T. Geerdes, *Zucker*, Stuttgarter Verlagskontor, 1963

H. C. Prinsen Geerligs, *The World's Cane Sugar Industry*, Norman Rodger, Altringham, 1912

W. E. Gros Clark, *History of the Primates*, University of Chicago Press, Chicago, 1966

W. Lutz, *Leben ohne Brot*, Selecta-Verlag, Munich, 1970

L. A. G. Strong, *The Story of Sugar*, George Weidenfeld and Nicolson, London, 1954

A. Viton and F. Pignalosa, *Trends and forces of world sugar consumption*, FAO Commodity Bulletin Series, No. 32, 1961

Selected Publications from Nutrition Department Queen Elizabeth College, London University

Books

T. C. Barker, J. C. McKenzie and J. Yudkin, *Our changing fare,* MacGibbon & Kee, London, 1966

T. C. Barker, D. J. Oddy and J. Yudkin, *The dietary studies of Dr. Edward Smith,* Staples, London, 1970

J. Yudkin, *This Slimming Business,* (3rd edition) Penguin, London, 1971

J. Yudkin and John C. McKenzie, *Changing food habits,* MacGibbon & Kee, London, 1964

J. Yudkin, J. Edelman and L. Hough, *Sugar,* Butterworth, London, 1971

Papers

John Yudkin, "Diet and coronary thrombosis. Hypothesis and Fact," *Lancet, II,* 155, 1957

John Yudkin, "The Epidemiology of coronary disease, Progress in Cardiovascular Diseases," *I,* 116, 1958

John Yudkin, "Etiology of cardiac infarction. A.M.A. Archives of Internal Medicine," *104,* 681, 1959

John Yudkin, "Diet and cardiac ischaemia. Proceedings of the 3rd International Congress of Dietetics: London 1961, 82," 1961

John Yudkin, "Fatty acids and coronary disease," *Practitioner, 187,* 150, 1961

John Yudkin, "Diet and the nation's health," *Journal of the Royal Society of Arts, 110,* 380, 1962

Ann M. Brown, J. C. McKenzie and John Yudkin, "Knowledge of nutrition amongst housewives in a London suburb," *Nutrition, 17,* 1, 1963

John Yudkin, "Nutrition and palatability with special reference to obesity, myocardial infarction, and other diseases of civilisation," *Lancet, I,* 1335, 1963

John Yudkin, "Dietary carbohydrate and ischemic heart disease," *American Heart Journal, 66*, 835, 1963

John Yudkin, "Dietary Fat and Dietary Sugar in Relation to Ischaemic Heart-Disease and Diabetes," *Lancet, II*, 4, 1964

John Yudkin and Janet Roddy, "Levels of dietary sucrose in patients with occlusive atherosclerotic disease," *Lancet, II*, 6, 1964

John Yudkin, "Patterns and trends in carbohydrate consumption and their relation to disease," *Proceedings of the Nutrition Society, 23*, 149, 1964

John Yudkin, "Sugar and coronary heart disease," *Food and Nutrition News, 36*, No. 6, 1965

John Yudkin, "Dietetic Aspects of Atherosclerosis," *Angiology, 17*, 127, 1966

John Yudkin, "Evolutionary and historical changes in dietary carbohydrates," *American Journal of Clinical Nutrition, 20*, 108, 1967

John Yudkin and Jill Morland, "Sugar Intake and Myocardial Infarction," *American Journal of Clinical Nutrition, 20*, 503, 1967

John Yudkin and Ronald Krauss, "Dietary Starch, Dietary Sucrose and Hepatic Pyruvate Kinase in Rats," *Nature, 215*, 75, 1967

D. G. G. Bett, Jill Morland and John Yudkin, "Sugar Consumption in Acne Vulgaris and Seborrhoeic Dermatitis," *British Medical Journal, 3*, 153, 1967

A. M. Cohen and John Yudkin, "The Effect of Dietary Sucrose Upon the Response to Sodium Tolbutamide in the Rat," *Biochimica et Biophysica Acta, 141*, 637, 1967

Stephen Szanto and John Yudkin, "The Effect of Dietary Sucrose on Blood Lipids, Serum Insulin, Platelet Adhesiveness and Body Weight in Human Volunteers," *Postgraduate Medical Journal, 45*, 602, 1969

John Yudkin, Stephen Szanto and V. V. Kakkar, "Sugar Intake, Serum Insulin and Platelet Adhesiveness in Men With and Without Peripheral Vascular Disease," *Postgraduate Medical Journal, 45*, 608, 1969

John Yudkin, "Sucrose and heart disease," *Nutrition Today, 4*, 16, 1969

Stephen Szanto and John Yudkin, "Dietary Sucrose and Platelet Behaviour," *Nature, 225*, 467, 1970

Sohair Al-Nagdy, D. S. Miller and John Yudkin, "Changes in

Body Composition and Metabolism Induced by Sucrose in the Rat," *Nutrition and Metabolism, 12,* 193, 1970

R. U. Qureshi, P. A. Akinyanju and John Yudkin, "The Effect of an 'Atherogenic' Diet Containing Starch or Sucrose Upon Carcass Composition and Plasma Lipids in the Rat," *Nutrition and Metabolism, 12,* 347, 1970

John Yudkin, "Sucrose, insulin and coronary heart disease," *American Heart Journal, 80,* 844, 1970

John Yudkin and Stephen Szanto, "Hyperinsulinism and Atherogenesis," *British Medical Journal, I,* 349, 1971

John Yudkin, "Nutrition and Atherosclerosis," *British Journal of Hospital Medicine, 5,* 665, 1971

John Yudkin, "A new look at diet and heart disease," *Cardiovascular Review,* 1971

K. R. Bruckdorfer, I. H. Khan and John Yudkin, "Dietary Carbohydrate and Fatty Acid Synthetase Activity in Rat Liver and Adipose Tissue," *Biochemical Journal, 123,* 7, 1971

Index

ABOUT THE AUTHOR

JOHN YUDKIN, M.D., Ph.D., is a physician, a biochemist, and currently Emeritus Professor of Nutrition at London University. Educated at London University, Cambridge University, and London Hospital Medical School, he was Professor of Physiology at Queen Elizabeth College of London University from 1945 to 1954 and Professor of Nutrition and Dietetics from 1954 to 1971. He is the author or co-author of five other books as well as thirty papers published in American and British scientific journals.

Exciting! Brand New!

Handy guides to personal success & happiness

Bantam Minibooks/50¢ each

There is a Bantam Minibook for almost every member of your family. These handy, compact, original books are written by renowned authorities—and they cost just 50¢ each!

- ☐ HAIRPIECES AND WIGS — (FX4205)
- ☐ DIET HATER'S DIET BOOK — (FX4210)
- ☐ SIMPLE ART OF MARRIED LOVE — (FX4304)
- ☐ NAME YOUR BABY — (FX4345)
- ☐ NO GUESS CALORIE COUNTER — (FX4356)
- ☐ SEWING WITHOUT A PATTERN — (FX4556)
- ☐ STOP DIETING! START LOSING! — (FX5297)
- ☐ YOGA U.S.A. — (FX4121)
- ☐ YOUR WEDDING — (FX4553)
- ☐ GAMES FOR COUPLES — (FX5293)
- ☐ HAIR DOS AND DON'TS — (FX4123)
- ☐ THE HOME BARTENDER'S GUIDE — (FX4561)
- ☐ QUICK KNITS FOR EVERYONE — (FX5292)
- ☐ BEAUTIFUL HAIR FOR EVERYONE — (FX4428)
- ☐ YOUR ENGAGEMENT — (FX5586)
- ☐ CREWEL EMBROIDERY SIMPLIFIED — (FX5974)

Buy them at your local bookstore or use this handy coupon for ordering:

Facts at Your Fingertips!

EUROPE, YOUR WAY!

These three helpful, matter-of-fact guides give you everything you need to know **before** you go! Whether it's your first trip or your fifty-first, these three guides tell you how to get the most out of Europe, your way!

THE REAL EUROPE AND THE MEDITERRANEAN (B7724/$2.25)
From what to see to where to shop, from where to sleep to what to eat, this is the MOST COMPREHENSIVE, UP-TO-DATE, all-inclusive guide to Europe and the Mediterranean, 1973!

THE REAL ECONOMY GUIDE TO EUROPE (Y7721/$1.95)
From how to stay in London for less than $5.00 a night to how to live in an Italian villa absolutely FREE! Here are hundreds of money-saving secrets to seeing Europe on **your** budget!

THE REAL RESTAURANT GUIDE TO EUROPE (Y7723/$1.95)
From the most elegant Parisian restaurants to enchanting inexpensive hideaways—here is the handiest, most complete guide to more than 200 great restaurants.